Praise for
Kingdom Woman

Hold onto something because *Kingdom Woman* will rock your world. If you're looking for a practical read that can help you leverage your purpose and power as a woman in the kingdom of God, look no further. This is the book for you! This book is for every woman who wants to serve God with substance and impact.

—Dr. Leslie Parrott
Author of *You Matter More Than You Think*

Kingdom Woman is inspiring, motivating, and catalyzing. Reading this book breathed life and refreshed faith into my heart. Women who want to live boldly and intentionally for the kingdom of God will find this book foundationally encouraging.

—Sally Clarkson
Author, popular conference speaker, and host of *itakejoy.com*

Never have women been bombarded with so many competing demands, choices, and expectations. In *Kingdom Woman* Dr. Tony Evans and Chrystal Evans Hurst inspire, equip, and empower us to believe God and with great faith to step up and into the purpose and plan He has for each one of our lives. Your kingdom contribution is important in every season. This book will help you to keep running your race beautifully.

—Christine Caine
Best-selling author of *Undaunted* and founder of The A21 Campaign

As I read *Kingdom Woman,* I recalled the beauty of a father waltzing with his daughter, admiring their graceful movements, and sensing their love and affection for each other. Their writing is poised with precision, capturing us with their compassion for God, family, each other and challenging each of us to learn to waltz with our heavenly Father as He leads and empowers us to live for Him.

—Sheila Bailey
Sheila B. Ministries

KINGDOM
WOMAN

TONY EVANS
CHRYSTAL EVANS HURST

KINGDOM WOMAN

EMBRACING YOUR PURPOSE,
POWER, AND POSSIBILITIES

TYNDALE HOUSE PUBLISHERS, INC.
CAROL STREAM, ILLINOIS

Kingdom Woman

Copyright © 2013 Tony Evans and Chrystal Evans Hurst

A Focus on the Family book published by Tyndale House Publishers, Inc., Carol Stream, Illinois 60188

Focus on the Family and the accompanying logo and design are federally registered trademarks of Focus on the Family, Colorado Springs, CO 80995.

TYNDALE and Tyndale's quill logo are registered trademarks of Tyndale House Publishers, Inc.

Cover design by Jennifer Ghionzoli
Cover skyline photo copyright © PhotoDisc. All rights reserved.
Cover photograph taken by Stephen Vosloo. Copyright © by Focus on the Family. All rights reserved.

Cataloging-in-Publication Data is available by contacting the Library of Congress at http://www.loc.gov/help/contact-general.html.

ISBN: 978-1-58997-743-3

Printed in the United States of America
2 3 4 5 6 7 8 9 / 17 16 15 14 13

There are four living generations of women in our family.
This book is dedicated to the three youngest:
Kariss
Jessica
Kelsey
—kingdom women in the making

CONTENTS

PART I: THE FOUNDATION OF A KINGDOM WOMAN
⌒ PURPOSE ⌒

PART II: THE FAITH OF A KINGDOM WOMAN
⌒ POWER ⌒

PART III: THE FRUIT OF A KINGDOM WOMAN
⌒ POSSIBILITIES ⌒

ACKNOWLEDGMENTS

I never imagined this life, one bursting at the seams with more goodness than any man could manage alone. Yet it has somehow been balanced with grace because of you, Lois. The greatest story in all the books of the world could never describe the affection and appreciation I have for you. Anything good I have ever accomplished has been because of you. What can I say, except thank you.

Chrystal, I was a twenty-two-year-old young man, steeped in inexperience, the very first time I laid eyes on you. The doctor came through the double doors into the waiting room where I'd been frantically pacing, and he told me you were here. And when I saw you, I knew I would never be the same again.

I could never have imagined that forty years later, you and I would sit down together, pens in hand, to write a book that would impact women everywhere. What a gift you have been to this project. What a gift you have been to me.

Tyndale and Focus on the Family: Finding publishers who carefully walk the fine line of ministry and business with grace and integrity can be a challenge. I've found that in you. Partnering with you on this book has been a joy. I can't wait to do it again soon.

Tony Evans

Daddy, thanks for the loving nudge in the direction of God's call on my life. You always see more in me than I do.

Mommy, I have had no better example than the one you have lived before my eyes, day in and day out, through the best and worst of times. So much of what I have learned about living as a kingdom woman, I have learned from watching you.

Kariss and Jessica, if you hadn't been willing to help me make dinner, clean up the kitchen, and watch your brothers, I wouldn't have had time to write. You are not just my daughters; you are my friends.

Silla, not a day goes by that I'm not grateful that you are my one and only sissy. I know I don't always act like it, but I'm glad when you walk over to my house and come in the back door without knocking. You are wonderful with words both spoken and written. Thanks for letting me learn from you.

Many thanks to Kanika, Michelle, and Wynter, who let me borrow their brains on a regular basis and granted me access to their insights and creativity. I appreciate every reply to my incessant e-mails, texts, and calls.

Sally Clarkson and Zan Tyler, your words of encouragement echo in my mind on a regular basis. Your words of affirmation watered dormant seeds and reminded me of who I am.

Andrea, you understand my life—homeschooling, housework, and hungry boys—so your reflections have meant so much. We will eventually make more time to hang out with our crew!

Focus on the Family and Tyndale House Publishers, thanks for the opportunity to work on a project with my dad.

And last but certainly not least, to my husband, Jessie, my kingdom man— you are the reason I have the freedom to find my path and try new things. Your deep and consistent love for this crazy wife God gave you makes my heart melt—over and over.

Chrystal

FOREWORD

A few women sighed in hesitation when we told them about this book. The thought of another manual to tell them what they aren't doing well and to give them instructions on how to change didn't sound appealing. The mere mention of a *kingdom woman* conjured up an idealistic image, one that instantly became a burden. Maybe, honestly, you feel the same way—a bit weary of having a finger waving in your face demanding that you do better—especially when you are already doing your absolute best.

We understand. Trust us, we understand—which is why we're glad you've opened this book.

This book, much like its companion *Kingdom Man*, will be unlike others you've read. It won't inform you and then leave you hanging to deal with a sense of condemnation and guilt. Every chapter will encourage and applaud you and then show you theologically and practically how to have the kind of faith that will usher in the miracle you've been looking for—the one you've been longing to see unfold in your family, church, or community. It will hand you a sword and then inspire you to draw it in the face of adversity instead of shrinking back into complacency or even into despair. After you take in these pages, you will be encouraged and you will also be empowered for the journey ahead.

Merging two unique messages into a succinct and singular package requires a pair of people who have walked through the annals of experience together. Our husband/father and daughter/sister are just the duo to make it happen. With Chrystal's frank, authentic, real-life perspective punctuating Tony's biblically inspired teaching, you will find this read an eye-opening and enlightening adventure through Scripture and then into your own heart.

Chrystal's a bit new on the publishing scene, but she shines in the women's ministry at our church and in our lives personally. For many years now, she has led the ladies of our local congregation, training them to be women of purpose who are equipped to reach their full potential. In a Christian world filled with folks striving for the limelight and a microphone, she has earned an esteemed place within the local church. That's something worth talking about. Her ability to engage and inspire an audience is compelling, but her faithfulness to disciple women one-on-one is admirable and has inspired others to do the same.

Even more impactful than that, Chrystal has managed to keep her priorities in place, structuring her time and efforts to focus primarily on her family. Honestly, we don't know how she does it, and we stand in awe of her every day. As a homeschool mother of five children, she knows the juggling act performed by millions of women the world over and has demonstrated what it means to honor God as a wife and mother. To top it off, she makes a loaf of homemade pumpkin bread that will make your mouth water.

In between washing dinner dishes, creating lesson plans, and taking the occasional field trip, Chrystal has managed to find time to blog her thoughts and life happenings in a way that has captured the attention of women. The treasure you will uncover in this manuscript will come not only from Tony's teaching but also from the story of Chrystal's life. Her deep, thriving relationship with Jesus is seen in every word, and her vulnerability and quick wit will draw you in and then cause you to see yourself in her life. You'll laugh at her stories and see the biblical truth she intended to share. Chrystal is refreshingly unassuming. Not perfect but purposeful. You won't feel pressured to emulate her, but you will want to walk alongside her.

Tony probably doesn't need any introduction. He has written more than sixty books, so the one you are holding in your hands is a continuation of a long line of fantastic titles. His contribution in publishing has blessed millions of people the world over and made an indelible mark on the health of the global church. His desire to uncover and then relay theological truths in a practical, relevant way has been the mark of his ministry—a ministry in which he has served his entire adult life. He is a faithful man who has dedicated himself to the Lord, his family, and the local church.

For more than three decades, he has pastored the same flock.

For more than four decades, he has loved the same wife.

For nearly five decades, he has taught the same unadulterated gospel of Jesus Christ. The depth of his integrity and character match the widespread reach of his ministry.

We wish we could have pulled you around our kitchen table to experience the after-dinner devotions that happened most nights in our home. Or invited you along for our yearly month-long road trip through the States that he courageously took us on each August. Or had you join us for Sunday-morning service where we've sat under his inspired teaching for thirty-seven years. Then you'd see the real man behind the larger-than-life persona—the introspective and loving pastor, father, and friend who has a heart that will resonate with yours through every portion of this book.

So, here's the deal: This book is like a train track headed to a destination that is worth every ounce of energy spent making the trip. And, like any track, this one has two rails bound together by the rungs of wisdom and experience. At different points in your journey, you'll need to be willing to hop on each one of these rails in order to get the most out of your reading. Each will allow you a different vantage point that will enhance the other. One side is Tony's—biblical, thought-provoking, and appropriately intense. It will require you to look into your Bible and then into your own soul as you learn lessons from ancient women that you may never have gathered before. Then Chrystal will beckon you over to her side of the track. You'll grab her hand, steady yourself on her rail, and begin a personal journey that will allow you to apply the truths you've been reading about.

We'll be honest and tell you that the ride won't always be easy and seamless. There might be some turns on a few steep spiritual cliffs that might make you feel like you won't make it to the other side intact—but you will.

You will.

Tony and Chrystal.

Father and daughter.

The perfect combination to bring you this incredible manuscript that will mark you forever. You'll emerge richer, wiser, and more motivated to become the kingdom woman you were created to be.

Be blessed as you read.

Lois Evans

Priscilla

THE SIGNIFICANCE OF A KINGDOM WOMAN

When a kingdom woman's alarm sounds each morning, the devil tries to hit her snooze button. He'll do whatever he can to try and stop her from getting up and taking on a new day.

Hell hath no fury like a kingdom woman disturbed. She won't stop doing all she can for the kingdom until she makes the devil regret ever messing with her.

As the strong and eloquent Eleanor Roosevelt once said, "A woman is like a teabag. You never know how strong it is until it's in hot water."[1] When the hot water comes, we often witness the explosion of strength and inner resolve that would put many men to shame. In childbirth alone, women frequently endure and experience more anguish and pain than scores of men sent out to war.

Women are often the unsung heroes behind any major victory, discovery, or moral campaign. Throughout history, when the men were away at battle, women held down the fort, assisted in creating and sending the supplies, ran the businesses, maintained the economy and community, and farmed—all while still managing their homes.

Women have always held a place of influence in culture, even if it hasn't been publicly recognized—or legally allowed. The nineteenth-century author Virginia Woolf wrote succinctly, "I would venture to guess that [Anonymous,] who wrote so many poems without signing them, was often a woman."[2] In fact, women have been equipped with such an innate capacity for influence that they can change the world for good or, unfortunately, for bad.

We are all too familiar with the negative influences. For example, Samson could defeat an entire army with the jaw of a donkey, but he became weak in the arms of one woman. Solomon had wisdom, riches, and power, but he still bowed to the ungodly influence of his many wives. David killed a giant with all the bravery and bravado of a gladiator—with only one stone and a slingshot. Yet King David was taken down by just one look at a bathing beauty.

Feminine influence doesn't solely come tied to sexuality, nor is it used only to gain a negative outcome. In fact, many women use their innate power to bring about good on behalf of those around them. Women in general mature faster than men, giving women an opportunity to make decisions in their earlier years that position them more securely in life and in the workplace. More women than men are graduating at all levels of college. And women's earnings have increased 56 percent on average since 1963, but their male coworkers are earning less than working men in 1970.[3]

> *Women have been equipped with such an innate capacity for influence that they can change the world for good.*

Not only are women influencing the workplace more than ever, but women are also often the impetus behind social change and transformation. The Center on Philanthropy found that women of the Baby Boomer generation and older, across nearly every economic bracket, give more—up to 89 percent more—to charity than men, thus raising the volume of their voices with regard to strategy, vision, and approach.[4]

Beyond that, women are gifted with a winsome ability to be disarmingly charming, even without using additional physical appeal. This alone can guide conversations their way, or influence major decisions in many realms, even unknowingly to those involved. Women also often embody additional spiritual depth and insight that captivate men because those qualities reflect something that men crave for themselves.

Our culture often displays a mirage that shows men having all the power, control, and influence. And men, in their most raw form, do seek to create, explore, build, exploit, achieve, and conquer, and then grab the glory for doing it all themselves. What is frequently missed: examining the motivation behind a man's ambitions, which is often the influence of a woman.

From early on, a man depends upon a woman in many ways—from the womb to early childhood, to teachers and the influence of media that creates an ideal image of a woman. A man doesn't buy a car just because he wants that fast-looking car. He will often buy a car to impress a woman, even if he won't admit that's why he did it.

Men often learn as early as junior high that the guys who play sports get the girls. The guys who drive nice cars, have money, or ooze charm get the girls. As they grow into men, those lessons stick with them as they aim for good jobs, a certain reputation, or success. All you have to do is listen to a song sung by a man to discover one of the biggest driving forces behind much of what men do. Here's an example you can find playing on today's radio stations, " 'Cause what you don't understand is I'd catch a grenade for ya."[5]

Our culture often displays a mirage that shows men having all the power, control, and influence.

Or from the soundtrack of the popular 1991 film *Robin Hood: Prince of Thieves,* a character of great gusto, power, and strength battles enemies in difficult and dangerous scenarios while the lyrics point to a woman being behind all his forays: "Everything I do, I do it for you."[6]

Or take it back to my generation with lyrics from the hit song "When a Man Loves a Woman" by the one and only Percy Sledge: "He'll trade the world for the good thing he has found."[7]

Rarely does an epic movie ever finish without somehow uniting or reuniting a man with a woman. Battles have been fought over women, history has been shaped by women, policy has been influenced or decided by women, nations have been run by women. Even in athletics women have power and influence. As recently as the London Olympics in 2012, American women won more *gold* medals not just over the American men but over most nations' *total* medal counts as well (China won thirty-eight and Great Britain tied the American women with twenty-nine). In fact, the United States women won a total of fifty-eight medals, which is more than sixty-four countries' total medal counts combined, not including China, Russia, and Great Britain.[8]

Sojourner Truth, one powerful woman, said, "If the first woman God ever made was strong enough to turn the world upside down all alone, these women together ought to be able to turn it back, and get it right side up again!"[9]

Eighteenth-century British essayist Samuel Johnson wrote at a time when women's rights were greatly limited by law, "Nature has given women so much power that the law has wisely given them very little."[10]

Thankfully, the legal rights and opportunities of women are no longer limited in America or many other countries as they were in the time of Virginia Woolf, Samuel Johnson, or Sojourner Truth, but the sentiment behind each of their statements remains true. Women are naturally gifted to influence and impact their world.

The First Woman

Women grace this planet with insight, sensitivity, and a spiritual beauty that has put them behind great accomplishments. The popular sayings ring true: The hand that rocks the cradle rules the world, and behind every great man is a greater woman. Or, in our case, behind every kingdom man is a kingdom woman. No one ever goes around saying, "Behind every great woman is a greater man." That phrase wouldn't fly. There are scores of single women who are successful, competent, and satisfied. And there are scores of married women whose husbands are clearly not kingdom men, yet those women remain every bit kingdom women themselves.

God has given women a diverse makeup that enables them to carry out multiple functions well.

God created man out of dust from the ground. At a basic level, the Creator picked up some dirt and threw Adam together. The Hebrew word for God forming man is *yatsar*,[11] which means "to form, as a potter." A pot usually has but one function.

Yet when God made a woman, He "made a woman from the rib he had taken out of the man" (Genesis 2:22). He created her with His own hands. He took His time crafting and molding her into multifaceted brilliance. The

Hebrew word used for making woman is *banah*, meaning to "build, as a house, a temple, a city, an altar."[12] The complexity implied by the term *banah* is worth noting. God has given women a diverse makeup that enables them to carry out multiple functions well. Adam may be considered Human Prototype 1.0, while Eve was Human Prototype 2.0.

Of high importance, though, is that Eve was fashioned *laterally* with Adam's rib. It was not a top-down formation of dominance or a bottom-up formation of subservience. Rather, Eve was an equally esteemed member of the human race.

After all, God spoke of the decision for their creation as one decision before we were ever even introduced to the process of their creation. The very first time we read about both Eve and Adam is when we read of the mandate of rulership given to both of them equally. We are introduced to both genders together, simultaneously. This comes in the first chapter of the Bible:

> Then God said, "Let us make man in our image, in our likeness, and let *them* rule over the fish of the sea and the birds of the air, over the livestock, over all the earth, and over all the creatures that move along the ground." So God created man in his own image, in the image of God he created him; male and female he created *them*. (Genesis 1:26–27)

Both men and women have been created equally in the image of God. While within that equality lie distinct and different roles (we will look at that in chapter 10), there is no difference in equality of being, value, or dignity between the genders. Both bear the responsibility of honoring the image in which they have been made. A woman made in the image of God should never settle for being treated as anything less than an image-bearer of the one true King. As Abraham Lincoln said, "Nothing stamped with the Divine image and likeness was sent in the world to be trodden on."[13]

Just as men, women were created to rule.

A Covenant for Dominion

When God created the heavens and the earth, He established an order. Although He is the Creator and the ultimate Ruler over His creation, He willingly empowered humankind to rule within His prescribed order. In theology this is known as the Dominion Covenant. It is where God turned over to men and women the immediate, tangible rule over His creation within the boundaries and stipulations that He has set forth. The Dominion Covenant is in Genesis 1 where we just read, "Then God said, 'Let us make man in our image, in our likeness, and *let them rule*'" (verse 26).

The Dominion Covenant is rarely taught or discussed. Yet it is no small thing. Fundamentally, it involves God's willing removal of Himself over the direct management of what He has created on earth while releasing that management responsibility to humankind.

When we read that God created man in His own image, both male and female were created. The Dominion Covenant applies not only to men, but also to women. A kingdom woman is an essential part of God's rule on earth. He has delegated this responsibility, empowering each of us to make decisions. These decisions come with blessings or consequences according to His boundaries and laws.

God has established a process whereby He honors our decisions—even if those decisions go against Him, or even if those decisions are not in the best interests of that which is being managed. God said, "Let *them* rule."

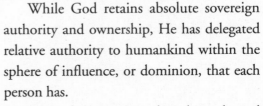

> *A kingdom woman is an essential part of God's rule on earth.*

While God retains absolute sovereign authority and ownership, He has delegated relative authority to humankind within the sphere of influence, or dominion, that each person has.

One of the reasons that this rule and management have been neglected to such a large degree is that many people are confused about why they are here on earth to begin with. This has happened because of a culture that has been flirting with hedonism for decades. A hedonistic worldview promotes the notion that someone's personal destiny exists to advance his or her personal happiness.

In God's economy, however, personal happiness is a derivative—a benefit—not the goal or driving force of destiny for a kingdom woman. Happiness is not *the* reason God created women. The reason He created women was to advance His kingdom and His glory.

Dominion in the Kingdom

God has invested His image in His men and women and placed them on display. A kingdom woman is to reflect Him and His kingdom in such a remarkable fashion that people want to know more about the kingdom she represents. She has been put here to reflect God's image.

I noticed an example of this while my wife, Lois, and I spent time in New York City this year. Every time we go, we inevitably stop by Saks Fifth Avenue for an afternoon. Display windows line the sidewalk outside so passers-by can catch a glimpse of what is inside the "kingdom" of Saks. The owners invest major time and resources to display what their kingdom has to offer.

I wish that more people realized how much God's kingdom has to offer. One reason so few people truly grasp the significance that comes from the Dominion Covenant is because they don't know the true value of God's kingdom. They don't know exactly what they have been placed here to represent.

The body of Christ, in general, focuses more on the concept of the church than on the kingdom. So many lives don't visibly demonstrate the significance God has given them. They don't advertise God's kingdom well.

One reason for that is the church has settled for buildings and programs instead of teaching men and women how to access the authority of the kingdom.

We've had church, but we haven't experienced the kingdom. Without our churches functioning in a kingdom-minded manner, believers are not being discipled to *be* the kingdom church that Christ came to build. In fact, Jesus only mentioned *church* three times in His earthly ministry, and all three times are recorded in the kingdom-focused book of Matthew.[14] The word *kingdom*, however, is found fifty-four times in the same book.[15]

We usually hear more about the church than the kingdom. We "plant churches" rather than promote the kingdom. Our seminaries teach our future leaders how to *do* church rather than how to *be* about the kingdom. Now, we can't have church without the kingdom, and the kingdom carries out its agenda through the church. Yet without an open and accurate teaching on how to live as kingdom men and women, we lack the direction to truly live out our destinies.

The Greek word for "kingdom" in the New Testament is *basileia*, which means "authority" and "rule."[16] A kingdom always includes three components: a ruler, a realm of subjects under its rule, and the rules or governances. The *kingdom of God* is the authoritative execution of *"His comprehensive rule over all creation."* The *kingdom agenda* is simply "the visible demonstration of the comprehensive rule of God over every area of life."[17]

God's kingdom transcends time, space, politics, denominations, cultures, and the realms of society. It is both now (Mark 1:15) and not yet (Matthew 16:28), close by (Luke 17:21) and removed (Matthew 7:21). The kingdom's realms include the individual, family, church, and civil government. God has given guidelines for the operation of all four, and neglecting these guidelines results in disorder and loss.

The main component upon which all else rests in a kingdom is the authority of the ruler. Without that, there is anarchy. Knowing this, Satan made sure that his first move was to try to subtly and deceitfully dethrone the Ruler by failing to use the term *LORD* as God did when He referred to Himself in the beginning of Genesis as *LORD God. Yahweh*, translated "LORD God" in the Bible, means "master, and absolute ruler"[18] and is the name God used to reveal Himself and His relationship to us. Prior to God revealing Himself to humans, He was introduced as Elohim, the powerful Creator.

> *A kingdom woman may be defined as a woman who positions herself under and operates according to the rule of God over every area of her life.*

When Satan spoke to Eve about eating the forbidden fruit, he did not refer to God as *LORD God*. Essentially, he stripped off the name *LORD* in Genesis 3:1: "Indeed, has *God* said . . . ?" (NASB). Satan tried to reduce God's rulership by beginning with a subtle but effective twist in His name. Satan's goal in doing so was to push Eve out from under God's kingdom definition and order.

When both Adam and Eve ate from the fruit in disobedience, they chose to change how they viewed God, removing the aspect of Master and Ruler. As a result, they lost their intimate fellowship with Him and with each other. Fortunately, on the cross Jesus Christ reintroduced this intimate fellowship through His sinless sacrifice and resurrection. We can enjoy unhindered fellowship with God now as a result of Christ's atonement. However, this only occurs when we align ourselves under God as *LORD God*—the Master and Ruler. Therefore, a *kingdom woman* may be defined as "a woman who positions herself under and operates according to the rule of God over every area of her life."

Eve didn't start out on such a great foot when she decided to act on her own rather than according to God's rule. Many women today still struggle with turning over personal control in their lives, thus opening themselves up to heartache, loss, and chaos. Yet because of the grace and mercy of Jesus Christ, any woman can align herself under God and experience a transformed life.

Chrystal's Chronicles

Kingdom woman. Those words sound like some pretty high stilettos to walk around in all day. The truth of the matter is that I know I'm not that woman. She is someone I strive to become but whose roles and responsibilities seem like a lot to handle. The very definition of a kingdom woman sets a high bar. After all, where is this woman—who is this woman—who regularly and consistently positions herself under and operates according to God's complete rule over her life?

Oh, I know. She must be my neighbor. She must be the woman who sits next to me at church or the lady who always seems to have the time to serve others. She must be the woman who has been married for fifty-seven years or the woman who is fifty-seven years old and has walked in remarkable purity. She must be the woman who walks with the tattered and torn Bible or the woman who keeps Jesus paraphernalia on her desk at work. She must be the woman who never yells at her kids and the woman who always cooks gourmet meals for her family. She must be the woman who has a work ethic beyond reproach and who lives in complete financial freedom because she regularly chooses frugality instead of fashion. She maintains a modest waistline and harbors no addictions. She must be every *other* woman, that is.

Just like Eve, we women tend to spend more time analyzing what we are not or what we don't have than recognizing who we were created to be. Satan's victory with Eve started way before she ate that fruit. The bite was only the culmination of a demise that began when Eve entered a conversation with the devil. And that's what we do a lot. We talk. We rehearse on a daily basis what we don't have or who we are not. We focus on the areas of our "garden" (our domain or our realm) that seem just out of our reach or control. We take the seed of discontentment offered by the devil and inform our souls of our dissatisfaction, unhappiness, or displeasure.

Just like Eve we have a choice. We can choose to believe what God's Word says about who we are and who we are created to be, or we can entertain the lies planted by the enemy of our souls and cultivated by the culture we live in. Romans 10:17 says that "faith comes from hearing the message, and the message is heard through the word of Christ." And that's what this book is about—hearing (and reading) what God says about who you are as a woman created for His glory.

You don't have to seek anyone else's approval for the life God has given you to live.

I desire to be the woman that He created me to be—not the woman whom I think I want to be or the woman the world tells me I should be. It brings me great joy to think of the detailed design and intricate effort that God put forth when making me. I'm so glad that I don't have to aspire to be anyone else other than that woman God wants me to be.

You don't have to seek anyone else's approval for the life God has given you to live. You don't have to apologize for the strength, fortitude, courage, talent, beauty, or intellect your Creator has given you. Ladies, we all are "God's workmanship, created in Christ Jesus to do good works, which God prepared in advance for us to do" (Ephesians 2:10).

Kingdom woman. Those four-inch red heels don't look easy to walk around in all day. But first looks can be deceiving. The right shoe made by the right designer and with the right materials can be not just wearable but comfortable! God has designed a plan and a purpose for you. You are not just "fearfully and wonderfully made" (Psalm 139:14); you are created in the image of a radiant, magnificent God who is full of beauty and splendor.

So wear His glory well. Walk on His runway.

More Than Helpers

An old saying goes, "Women who seek to be equal with men lack ambition." Think about that for a second, because I don't want you to miss the potency of its point. So many women have been taught that because God deemed woman as a "helper" for Adam, women are consequently "less than" men. Women often hear that they are to be like the Holy Spirit in His role of "helper." Yet a closer look at the Hebrew word used for "helper" in Scripture should be eye-opening for you.

The Hebrew words translated "helper suitable for him" in the creation story are important because they're surprisingly powerful. They are *ezer* and *kenegdo*. The word *ezer* occurs twenty-one times in the Old Testament, with only two of those times referring to a woman. The remaining usages refer to help that comes directly from God the Father.[19]

Here are some examples:

There is none like unto the God of Jeshurun, who rideth upon the heaven in thy help *[ezer]*. (Deuteronomy 33:26, KJV)

Our soul waiteth for the LORD: he is our help *[ezer]* and our shield. (Psalm 33:20, KJV)

Yet I am poor and needy; come quickly to me, O God. You are my help *[ezer]*. (Psalm 70:5)

Our help *[ezer]* is in the name of the LORD. (Psalm 124:8)

To distinguish *ezer* from every other Old Testament use, which referred to a stronger help brought by God, the word *kenegdo* was added. It literally means "before your face, in your view, or purpose."[20] Some have translated *kenegdo* to also mean "a completion of" or "counterpart to." As you can see from the name that God gave to Eve, hers isn't a role of subservience, maid service, or even that of being a slave. Hers is a strong help comparable to that of God the Father.

Many people see the Bible as a book written with a pessimistic or dismissive view of women. Charles Templeton, who was once an evangelist and then began doubting the Bible, succinctly stated this opinion in *Farewell to God:* "In the Bible women are secondary creatures and relatively unimportant" and "In the majority of the basic expressions of Christianity, women remain subject to and secondary to men."[21] Those, like Templeton, who feel that Scripture was created as a reflection of a misogynist worldview that oppress and negates the value of women clearly haven't looked at the original language and context.

Yet the very word God chose to use for woman's purpose and intention is the same word used to refer to Himself as the primary person in the Godhead. God does not shy away from referring to Himself or defining Himself through the use of feminine terms or imagery. Some examples include the following:

- God like a woman in labor (Isaiah 42:14)
- God like a midwife (Psalm 22:9–10; 71:6; Isaiah 66:9)
- God like a woman seeking a lost coin (Luke 15:8–10)
- God like a mother bear (Hosea 13:8)
- God like a mother:
  - nursing her children (Numbers 11:12)
  - not forgetting her children (Isaiah 49:14–15)
  - comforting her children (Isaiah 66:13)
  - birthing and protecting Israel (Isaiah 46:3–4)
  - calling, holding, healing, and feeding her children (Hosea 11:1–4)
  - gathering her children like a mother hen (Matthew 23:37)
  - protecting her young (Psalm 17:8; 36:7; 57:1; 91:1–4)

In fact, not only does God use feminine terminology and imagery to communicate major spiritual principles, but the primary reference to the church throughout Scripture is also made with feminine terminology (for example, the bride of Christ).

When Jesus chose to use Mary as an example of personal discipleship,

He affirmed her in a way that was contrary to the cultural norms of that day for women. Rather than uphold the cultural expectation that women ought to be about housework in the kitchen, as Martha was doing, Jesus specifically stated that Mary had chosen the better thing by engaging in theological study at the feet of Christ, which was solely the practice of men learning at the feet of a rabbi in that day. Jesus Christ not only esteemed Mary's decision as a woman, but He also commended it.

God holds women in such high regard that He will not even listen to a man's prayers when he does not honor her as an equal heir in God's kingdom.

In fact, God holds women in such high regard that He will not even listen to a man's prayers when he does not honor her as an equal heir in God's kingdom (1 Peter 3:7).

God Created Woman; Adam Did Not

God's creation of woman was not the result of Adam's request. It wasn't Adam who said he needed someone in his life. Rather, God said it: "It is not good that the man should be alone" (Genesis 2:18, KJV). God saw the apparent need for a partner to fulfill the Dominion Covenant, so He created an *ezer kenegdo*. Adam took no part in the creation of Eve other than taking a nap.

Eve's first calling was to God—to fulfill His purpose for her life, which in her case was to help Adam. Her role as helpmate was not just a role of companionship; it also included a significant role as collaborator in the dominion mandate.

Yet many women today—either because of divorce or a lack of kingdom men to even marry—do not have an Adam to help. If you are one of these women, take courage and pride in your calling, because God alone is your purpose. You have been made for Him. As He said in Isaiah,

"For your Maker is your husband—the LORD Almighty is his name—
the Holy One of Israel is your Redeemer; he is called the God of all the

earth. The LORD will call you back as if you were a wife deserted and distressed in spirit—a wife who married young, only to be rejected," says your God. (54:5–6)

Whether you are married on earth or if God is your Husband (Isaiah 54:5), your worth is far above any treasure. One of the most important truths you need to believe concerns your worth. You are significant. You are valuable. You are worth more than jewels. As a kingdom woman who fears the Lord, guard your value by first making sure you view yourself according to the value God has given to you. You are to do all you can to ensure that others treat you with dignity. You are to be treated as a treasure, not as someone to be trashed or used.

> *A kingdom woman succeeds in conquering the Enemy's attempts to mess with her life and the lives of the people she loves.*

I understand that there are situations where you may not be able to control how you are treated, but that doesn't mean you have to acquiesce to it. You do not have to internally accept someone else's denigration of you. It should not affect your view of who you are. As Eleanor Roosevelt said, "No one can make you feel inferior without your consent."[22]

You are first and foremost a kingdom woman created for God's work. Your life, through His sustaining strength, ought to be one of great purpose, spiritual power, and possibilities.

When a kingdom woman retires for the evening, a frustrated and worn-out devil ought to be saying, "I messed with the wrong woman today." There is nothing like a kingdom woman who succeeds in conquering the enemy's attempts to mess with her life and the lives of the people she loves. There is nothing like a kingdom woman who succeeds in finding and fulfilling the purpose for which God has fashioned her.

There is nothing like a kingdom woman fully formed.

PART I

THE FOUNDATION OF A KINGDOM WOMAN PURPOSE

1

A WOMAN OF VALUE

When a kingdom woman begins her day, heaven, earth, and hell take notice. When she nurtures and advises the man she loves, he can do little to resist her. When she offers care, comfort, and encouragement to her friends and relatives, they are able to go farther, faster, and in confidence because of her inspiration and reassurance. "Her children rise up and call her blessed" (Proverbs 31:28, ESV). Other women turn to her for wise counsel and a compassionate ear. Her church relies on her faithful service. She is a vital contributor to culture and a gatekeeper at her home to keep out the negative and promote the positive.

When we examine the history of the Christian faith, kingdom women (both married and single) are everywhere. Kingdom women throughout the Bible saved lives and nations. It was Jochebed who intervened on behalf of her son Moses (Exodus 2). Because of her watchful protection, Moses was later used as the deliverer of Israel (Exodus 3). It was Moses' wife, Zipporah, who saved Moses' life when God was going to punish him for his refusal to follow a simple command (Exodus 4:24–26). Esther's bravery gave the opportunity for the Jewish people to defend themselves from what would have been utter annihilation (Esther 7–8). Ruth's refusal to return to her own people because of her dedication to her mother-in-law, Naomi, led to the ongoing line of the Messiah (Ruth 4:18–22). Rahab was instrumental in the victory of Israel over Jericho (Joshua 2). Mary carried God's Son in her womb (Luke 1:30–35).

The clearest profile of a kingdom woman that I have ever found in the Bible is in Proverbs 31. What is interesting, though, is that in all of my study of Scripture, I have never found a corollary passage for men as Proverbs 31 is for women. It could be that men need the whole Bible to get it right, while women just need a chapter.

The Proverbs 31 woman is the hallmark of kingdom women. I like to call her a woman for all seasons. She is strong, intelligent, capable, giving, resourceful, efficient, spiritually minded, and much more.

Now, don't close this book just yet. I know that sounds like she is a perfect woman, and you may feel that her standard is set too high to actually reach. But the Proverbs 31 woman is not the model of a perfect woman. Neither is a kingdom woman called to perfection.

> *The Proverbs 31 woman is not the model of a perfect woman. Neither is a kingdom woman called to perfection.*

Let's use a stay-at-home mom as just one example. A kingdom woman is not someone who can multitask perfectly while also homeschooling three very different children, serving on four church committees, carpooling eleven neighborhood kids back and forth to soccer, keeping her home spotless, coaching the spelling-bee team, functioning as a killer CEO in the workplace, making her husband have the best night of his life each and every evening, and maintaining a size 6 figure well into her fifties—all while cooking only organic, nongenetically modified foods and making every meal from scratch.

That woman doesn't exist. And we didn't put this book together to make you think that you should be her either. In fact, from my experience pastoring a church for nearly four decades and spending thousands of hours counseling both women and men, the issue is often that women are trying to do too much—and all at once.

Women, you can be a Proverbs 31 woman and more—but that doesn't mean you do it all at the same time.

One of the most important principles for you as a kingdom woman is that your life flows through different seasons. Each of these seasons carries with it different time constraints, blessings, and demands. To try to do all things without being cognizant of the season you are in is the surest way to burnout and even bitterness.

The primary foundation of being a kingdom woman doesn't include a million different things done a million different ways. The primary foundation is actually simple and straightforward. It is located at the end of Proverbs 31. After listing everything that this particular woman did, the verse says,

> Charm is deceptive, and beauty is fleeting;
>> but a woman who fears the LORD is to be praised.
> Give her the reward she has earned,
>> and let her works bring her praise at the city gate. (Verses 30–31)

What sets a kingdom woman apart from any other woman boils down to her fear of God. Her reverence determines her actions, thoughts, words, and priorities. Without that, the demands of life would overwhelm any woman.

Fear the Lord

A woman who fears the Lord will receive the praise that is due her. Her works and the products of her hands will give her the recognition and validation that are hers alone. When a woman understands who she is and how God made her—when she pursues her destiny in light of how God created her to function—what she does will produce remarkable results. This is because it will be in line with God's will. What too many women frequently do is base their decisions on trying to please others, or trying to earn acceptance, appreciation, or a sense of worth from their decisions, appearance, or actions. Yet God never said that you would receive praise for trying to please others.

The primary influence in a kingdom woman's life is God. His voice is the loudest. He is the One she seeks to please.

The basis of how a kingdom woman functions comes out of her fear of God. How she prioritizes her home and family, organizes her life, makes decisions, chooses investments, and develops her skills occurs from her efforts to advance God's kingdom. If her priorities are rooted in anything else, they will lead to weariness and busyness rather than fruitfulness and abundance.

The simplest way I know to define what it means to fear God is to take God seriously. It means to place what God says and what God requires as the highest priority in your life. Fearing God does not mean that you are scared of Him. Fear is better understood as reverence or awe. It means to hold in highest esteem. A kingdom woman fears the Lord in every area of her life.

The marketplace does not control a woman who fears God. The television, magazines, blogs, and social media sites do not influence her away from Him. Her friends don't dictate her emotions or decisions. The culture doesn't define her. Even her own ambitions don't dominate her. Rather, the primary influence in a kingdom woman's life is God. His voice is the loudest. He is the One she seeks to please. Her reverence of Him determines her choices.

The Results of Fearing God

Yes, the Proverbs 31 woman did a lot. She earned her husband's trust, she made clothes for her family, she got her food from the choicest providers, and she invested in a small business with her earnings from planting a vineyard. She helped the poor, took care of those within her home, and dressed herself and her children in quality clothes. She brought respect to her husband and wisdom to those around her.

Keep in mind, she lived in a day and a culture where planting a vineyard did not mean that she did it all on her own. The passage said her arms were strong (verse 17), so we know she did do some of it. But based on the cultural norms of the day, it is likely that she hired others to work in her vineyard. She would have had maidservants who helped around the home, washed clothes, prepared food, and more.

When you break down all that the Proverbs 31 woman did and translate it into contemporary times, it really doesn't sound as lofty and unattainable. Essentially, she honored and respected her husband. She fed and clothed her family with the healthiest and finest she could afford. She invested the use of her skills in a personal business, spoke wisely and kindly to others, dressed herself attractively, and helped the poor. All of those actions can easily translate into your world today.

I don't want you to feel that what she attained is so far out of reach from what God is able to do through you. Because it's not. What it comes down to is that her fear and reverence for God caused her to do the best she could with what she had to promote God's kingdom and goodness in her own life and the lives of those around her.

Help Is Not Bad

An important principle that is often overlooked when we examine the life of the Proverbs 31 woman is that she was not too proud to get help. In verse 15 we read, "She gets up while it is still dark; she provides food for her family and portions for her servant girls." *Servant girls* is not a term that we use today. In ancient Hebrew society, it referred to a handmaid or helper. It is a small reference to a very important truth. As I mentioned earlier, the kingdom woman in Proverbs 31 didn't try to do it all on her own. She had help. She was diligent, resourceful, and productive, yet she didn't do it all alone.

For some reason people have come to believe that "exhaustion is close to godliness" is written somewhere in the Bible.

There is a stigma today for Christian women in particular about asking for or using help. For some reason people have come to believe that "exhaustion is close to godliness" is written somewhere in the Bible. It is not. The fastest way to get yourself off track from fulfilling God's kingdom destiny for you is to view yourself as a superwoman who has to do it all on her own. The key to your destiny is humbly acknowledging your dependence on God and maximizing all He provides you, even if that includes accepting or using the help of others.

For example, in the corporate world, a manager would not be considered a great manager if she tried to do everyone's job herself. A great manager knows how to draw out the best from those around her while simultaneously leading and complementing their efforts. You don't have to achieve your destiny alone.

Chrystal's Chronicles

I was crashing and crashing fast. After a wild holiday season followed by a trip out of state for our son's surgery, I felt as if my household was spinning out of control. At the time I had a teenager, a preteen, a preschooler, a toddler, and an infant. Oh, and did I mention a loving kingdom man as a husband who just so happened to work in the music business, which meant a lot of travel and time away managing concert tours? I was sleep deprived, short on energy, and short on hours.

Looking around my house, I knew I couldn't do it all. But I was determined to try. I was convinced that I shouldn't need assistance with my duties as a wife and mother. I'd always worked well under pressure and been able to keep a few plates spinning at the same time. Having been a mother from the early age of nineteen, I knew what it was like to juggle priorities and commitments to get everything done. I liked being capable, and I definitely didn't want anyone else in the picture to get the glory, uh . . . I mean . . . be burdened with responsibilities that were supposed to be mine.

I would see other women who I just *knew* were superwomen and didn't ask for help. Little did I know that some of them were dropping their spinning plates too! We know how to mask things, don't we? Each of us in our own manner finds a way to make things look nice and tidy to outsiders while we know the truth about the mess behind closed doors.

I wasn't ready to admit that I needed help. I wanted to be superwoman too.

I remember one night of that crazy-busy season, in those wee, honest hours, sometime after the last child fell sleep and my husband dozed off, there was no sound except for the still, small voice of God wondering in a whisper if He had somehow been forgotten that day. I prayed with a metaphorical hand on my hip. "God," I said, "if You want me to have time for You, too, then I need some help getting things done. And I need *You* to bring help to *me*." I didn't want to have to humble myself so much to actually go look for help—therefore acknowledging that I needed some.

But that's how great God is. Despite my ornery self, He heard my prayer in the middle of my dark and overwhelming night.

Now before I share the answer to that prayer with you, let me tell you about my philosophy on cleaning. I abide by the saying, "My house should be clean enough to be healthy, but messy enough to be lived in." Because I homeschool our children, I don't ever expect my home to look like it came out of a magazine. I—along with four to five children (depending on the time of year)—am home at least four days a week all day. My house isn't going to stay pristine just because I clean all the time. Not possible. I strive for balance between being a good mom, teacher, cook, wife, and homemaker. I'll trade a random opportunity to bounce around on the trampoline with my kids over scrubbing the baseboards any day!

Sure, I know a handful of ladies who are good housekeepers, great housekeepers, in fact. I have tried to figure out with my husband how they do it. Here is what I have learned. We all have the same twenty-four hours in a day. If someone else's home is always pristine, it has to do with how she spends her time. My friend with the beautiful home and four homeschooled children has children all over the age of twelve. (Do you hear that, moms of small children? She has no little people!) Sure, she is running around to basketball and soccer practice, but with four other capable bodies in the house, she also has lots of help. Another friend of mine with small children has a gorgeous magazine-ready home. But her children spend three days a week at a Mother's Day Out . . . and she has a nanny. My friend who makes gourmet meals every night has her kids in traditional school all day.

I also have a friend whose home is always in disarray, but she enjoys her little children and plays with them quite a bit more than I play with mine. They are always outside playing or inside working on some neat craft. Creativity and fun are their family's highest values in their current season. Ladies, it's all about how God designed you and what is important in your life right now. That determines how you choose to spend your time. No one can do it all.

So as a mom in the middle of mothering preschoolers on up to young adults, I just do my best. If I tried to put housework first at all costs, something else that is important would suffer: building relationships with my children.

As a result of my revelation, I have gone through a series of adjustments in my personal expectations over the last few years so that I can stay sane.

A few of my compromises are as follows:

- I aim for a clean kitchen twice a day. Three times is a luxury. Even so, I always expect there to be dishes in the sink.

- I shoot for a mopped floor two times a week, unless otherwise necessary. It's just too depressing to mop the floor only to find in just a few hours that it doesn't look like I did anything.
- I try to hit each room in my house once a week on a rotating schedule. What does this mean? My house is not clean all at the same time.
- I'm constantly training my children to care for our home, because I'm trying to work myself out of a job. This means our "clean home" is not going to be perfectly clean.
- Laundry is always going. I do about a load a day.
- My carpet is never going to look new, no matter how many rules I make about food and drink staying in the kitchen. It just doesn't happen. What can I say?
- We *live* in our home. My teenager does schoolwork at the computer, my little ones do schoolwork at the kitchen table, we congregate at the island— in short, we are all over the place. As we transition to the dinner hour, I shoot for things in their place. If I can't have that, then I shoot for neat piles.
- Oh, and the baseboards? I get to 'em when I get to 'em. (Or I'll just wait until my little ones are old enough to do a good job—they are nearer to the floor anyway!)

But here's my problem. I am comfortable with the standards in my home. But when I have a visitor, I'm still completely thrown into a panic. Why? Because I don't want to leave a bad impression of the kind of housekeeper I am!

So imagine my dismay when my dad showed up for an unannounced visit and proceeded to inspect my house. I kid you not; he went from room to room, each time saying, "Oh, Chrystal!" This coming from a man who barely raises his voice (except to preach, of course). Now, granted, the day he came was a bad day. Forget all my housekeeping rules. He wouldn't have known I had any!

In fact, it was a Monday. Mondays are always the worst. He commented on the spots on the carpet, the dishes in the sink, the stuff on my countertops, and the baskets of unfolded clothes in the hallway, and then he even peeked in my bedroom and saw the confusion in there. When he looked in my refrigerator, Dad groaned at the sticky stuff on the top shelf too.

I found myself following him around the house, explaining, explaining, and explaining some more.

So, how does the story end? Well, the Lord sent me help. My dad lovingly told me that I shouldn't try to do it all and that it wasn't a bad thing to have some help every now and then, especially for a mother of five children. He offered to send over a housekeeping service. He also told me to get my carpets cleaned at his expense.

Now, I have a lot of pride. I hate the idea that I can't do it all. I hate accepting help. The truth is, though, that I needed and appreciated the boost he provided. It saved me hours (probably days) of work and gave me an opportunity to focus on things that needed my personal attention.

Now, I have a lot of pride. I hate the idea that I can't do it all. I hate accepting help.

I had time to catch up on balancing our bank account and plan ahead for school. Instead of doing dishes, I was able to make some much-needed phone calls to insurance companies and doctors. I got a chance to scrub that graffiti off the side of my house (long story on that one). I had lots of time to thoroughly finish planning for my daughter's upcoming birthday. Those are things a cleaning service can't do, but I *could*. That little injection of more available time in my schedule got me going. I started barreling through my list and got caught up in getting things *done*!

The point of this little illustration is not to say that everyone ought to dig into her pockets to pay someone to clean her home all the time or even every now and then, for that matter. The principle here is that you and I don't have to do it all. The Proverbs 31 woman didn't.

She lived in a culture where children were instrumental in carrying out large duties from a very young age. (Put those kids to work!) She did not peel those carrots or cut those potatoes all by herself. She probably did not make all the trips to the market for food and cloth herself. (There's nothing wrong with shopping online, girls!) The field she bought was probably researched and recommended by a trusted friend. (Use the expertise of others, honey!) And she did have "maidens." Ladies, if you are in a position to curb some of the wants in your budget (shopping, cell phone, cable, eating out, hair, etc.) so that you can hire a housekeeping service once a month—therefore helping you be a kinder, gentler person—by all means, do it! The Proverbs 31 woman did a lot, yes. But she did it with help. And that makes all the difference in the world.

The picture of the Proverbs 31 woman should never make us feel guilty. Okay, maybe we can agree that she was a woman who had it all . . . but let's also agree that she didn't have it all at the same time. Proverbs 31:10–31 summarizes her whole life.

Becoming a Proverbs 31 woman is not unattainable, but she definitely is a model of a woman we can emulate if we take the time to get to know her. The Proverbs 31 woman keeps her priorities straight and in line with God's priorities for her. She maximizes her gifts and uses everything and everyone at her disposal. She is a manager. She doesn't do it on her own.

As a recovering do-it-all-aholic, I am right there with you in letting those unrealistic expectations go.

Let yourself off the hook. Find out what God is doing, jump in the river of His will, and flow with the current of His plans. Accept help when it is offered from a friend, a family member, a church member, a coworker, or even a stranger. You do not have to do all, be all, and have all, all at the same time. There are other people, right now in your home, at your job, in your church, and in your community, who can do a good job too. Share the load. We need to get off the I-can-do-it-all kick.

As a recovering do-it-all-aholic, I am right there with you in letting those unrealistic expectations go. Rest in the Lord's expectations for you. He knows what you need, and He loves you greatly. He answered my prayer at dark-thirty when I told Him I just couldn't do it all. He said, "Chrystal, I know that. I've been waiting a long time for you to know that too."

Remember Martha and Mary? It is so easy for us as women to focus on the *doing* rather than on the most important thing—*being* in a vibrant relationship with our Savior.

Cooking and cleaning are important . . .

Raising your children is important . . .

Cultivating a healthy marriage is important . . .

Doing a good job and building a career are important . . .

Contributing in your community is important . . .

Exercising wisdom in your finances is important . . .

Serving in your church is important . . .

Taking care of your health is important . . .

Spending quality time with friends and family is important . . .

Enjoying your life is important . . .

But none of those things should ever be a stumbling block that keeps you from fearing God, finding out what His priority is for you, and focusing on what matters for eternity.

Fearing God means that His program is your program. His plan is your plan. And His purposes are the purposes you live to fulfill.

Fearing God means that you are clear on the idea that your life is actually His life—that He is living through *you*.

A wise mentor once shared this thought with me: "Each morning before you allow your feet to hit the floor, lie in bed for one purposeful moment longer than you normally would, stretch your arms toward the ceiling and in effect toward heaven, and offer yourself to the Lord, inviting Him to show you what the most important thing is on His list for you to get done today. If you do not stop to ask Him what His priorities are for you, your "good" will always get in the way of God's "best." Let Him know that you are willing to be interrupted, willing to be derailed, and willing to be surprised if He sees fit. Then get up and walk in the knowledge that your day belongs to the Lord."

We are all in different seasons of life, with different responsibilities, demands, and distractions. But no matter our season, God sees us where we are, and He hears our prayers in the middle of our dark and overwhelming nights—even when we pray with our hands on our hips.

The best news is that when you are a kingdom woman who chooses to walk in the fear of the Lord, then it's His job to find and provide the tools you need to get His work done!

God Is Your Biggest Helper

Chrystal's illustration might sound familiar to you. Maybe you've been there. Maybe you've gotten to the point where you wonder how you are supposed to do it all. But the lesson Chrystal learned and the help she accepted is a lesson for you as well. Wisdom entails recognizing what season you are in and living according to that. Never be ashamed to admit that you can't do it all. The main thing is that you keep God first and foremost, and His strength will give you what you need to make decisions that will glorify Him.

While the Proverbs 31 kingdom woman serves as the ideal, the reality of day-to-day life for a woman—whether caring for children or parents, holding down a job, taking care of her home, and even taking care of herself—might make that ideal seem impossible. But the goal is to let the fear of God be the overriding influence in your life. Let your actions, thoughts, and words reflect a heart that seeks to honor Him above all else. As you do, God will continue to give you what you need to develop into the kingdom woman you are destined to be.

Like Chrystal, when you call out to Him, He will send you help:

> I lift up my eyes to the hills—
>   where does my help come from?
> My help comes from the LORD,
>   the Maker of heaven and earth. (Psalm 121:1–2)

When you ask Him for wisdom, He promises to give it: "If any of you lacks wisdom, he should ask God, who gives generously to all without finding fault, and it will be given to him" (James 1:5).

Reverence for God serves as the foundation upon which your significance as a kingdom woman will flourish.

He will never leave you. He has not abandoned you. In fact, He wants to see you develop into the kingdom woman He designed you to be even more than you may want to. God has a plan for you, and at times—I know—that plan may feel overwhelming. You may not see how you could ever get to next week, let alone through this year. Your plate is full, your energy is low, and the call to be a kingdom woman seems lofty.

But I want you to start right here with this very simple principle from Proverbs 31: Fear God in all you do. Honor Him with your heart, thoughts, words, and actions. Seek Him, look to Him, and accept the help He brings your way. Take your life one day at a time. Honor and revere Him today. Fear Him in everything. Demonstrate that reverence through all you do. If you will do that, you will be on your way to being a kingdom woman living out her destiny. Reverence for God serves as the foundation upon which your significance as a kingdom woman will flourish.

2

A WOMAN OF HOPE

There's a beautiful story about a beautiful lady. Her name was Cinderella. But Cinderella felt ugly. She lived with a wicked stepmother and two equally wicked stepsisters. They made Cinderella their slave. Now, she was beautiful, but she didn't think about herself as beautiful, because of the influence of a wicked environment that put her down, messed her over, and reduced her to nothing. The problem with Cinderella was that she was stuck there. She was locked in the situation, and for a long time she could not get out of it.

You've heard the story. You know about the ball and how she was miraculously transported there in a carriage. At that ball she met a prince. The prince saw Cinderella and loved her. But the problem in the story, as you know, is that the clock struck midnight, and she reverted to her old self. She became a slave again to an evil family.

The good part of Cinderella's story, though, is that the prince never forgot her. Even though a lot of people had been at the ball, something about Cinderella made her stand out from the crowd. She was special. She was unique. She was rare. Everyone wanted the prince, but the prince wanted Cinderella.

All he had to work with to find her, though, was a shoe she had left behind. If he could find the foot that fit the shoe, he would find Cinderella. So he set out going house to house in search of his treasure. After a long and hard search, the prince finally found her.

A lot of women today are living like Cinderella. They are influenced by a wicked stepmother—the Devil, who's got two wicked daughters: the world and the flesh. Living as slaves in a hostage situation, many women feel trapped in a hopeless scenario. Perhaps this describes you in some way. Maybe you thought you would be further along than you are right now. Maybe you had a brighter dream for how your family would be, or your career, or your relationships. Maybe you even met the Prince of Peace, and He saved you some time ago, but you have found yourself again in bondage. That could mean emotional bondage, spiritual bondage, or even physical bondage.

> *Jesus knows right where you are, and He knows how long you've been there.*

It is easy to lose heart when you can't see an end to the tyranny. What I want to remind you is that there is hope. Jesus knows right where you are, and He knows how long you've been there. He has a way out of any hopelessness you may feel.

He doesn't just want to bring His money to you, His castle to you, or His chariot to you. He wants to bring you to Him. He wants to take you out of the bondage and let you live in the freedom of His presence and provision. He wants to show you your new position and your new glory. He wants to get you out of a spirit of slavery. He wants to give you hope.

Suppose Cinderella had given up. Suppose she had resolved to stay locked away in the house. She would never have been found by the prince. She would never have tried on her own shoe. She would have missed out on happily ever after.

A lot of us have given up on God. We have counted the years when it seems our prayers have not been answered, and we have determined it's too late. Too many times we miss out on the destiny God has for us because we have stopped looking. We have stopped hoping.

Scripture has another story for us of a woman limited by bondage. She wasn't Cinderella, but she faced her own ongoing struggles that kept her from living out the truest form of her destiny. This woman who was unable to stand tall is in the book of Luke. It says, "A woman was there [in the synagogue] who had been crippled by a spirit for eighteen years. She was bent over and could not straighten up at all" (13:11).

Here we have a woman who for eighteen years had an unfixable problem that doubled her over. Like the hunchback of Notre Dame, she could not straighten up. Her eyes regularly saw only the ground because she was unable to look elsewhere. The passage makes it plain that there was nothing she or anyone else could do to straighten things up for her. She perhaps had some kind of spinal deformity that kept her bent over.

Because of her physical position, she could never fully see things as they really were. Her perception not only of herself but also of the world around her was distorted. Her issue was not just one of health, but it had become one of habit simply because it had gone on for so long. Eighteen years is a long time to have your world affected adversely by something you did nothing to deserve and have no power to change. This woman's life had to have been filled with discouragement day after day, week after week, month after month, year after year. It would be easy to assume that the woman may have lost her hope.

Are you able to identify with her—or with Cinderella—in any way? Maybe you have experienced a pain or a problem that won't go away, and you feel stuck in a rut. Or stuck in a position that doesn't offer any hope for a brighter tomorrow. While this woman's issue was physical, many trials can force your head or heart downward either emotionally or spiritually. It could be something your dad said or did, or even your mom. It could be something an unthinking sibling might have done or said that has kept you emotionally crippled for so long. It could even be a spouse, friends, or people at work who have mislabeled you and held you back from your destiny as a kingdom woman.

You've tried reading books to set yourself free, attending Bible studies, and talking to a counselor, pastor, or friends, but no matter what you do, the problem or bondage seems to remain. The first thing I want to tell you is that you are not alone. Many women feel bound by emotional, spiritual, or physical pain. It could be that you feel you've followed God's Word and honored Him with your life, but somehow He hasn't held up His end of the bargain. Whatever it is, it has you downcast. And whatever has you downcast has distorted your perception not only about yourself but also about the world around you.

Before you give up, though, look up.

See, being a kingdom woman isn't summed up in just going to church more or doing more good things. It's about connecting with the One who gives hope. Luke 13 tells us that the lady who couldn't straighten up was in the synagogue. She was at church: "On a Sabbath Jesus was teaching in one of the synagogues . . . " (verse 10). For eighteen years, this woman most likely had come to church, sung her songs, listened to sermons, praised God, given her alms, and more. Yet she was no further along in being set free from her bondage than the first day she had come. Evidently church, in and of itself, didn't help her. The system of religion, in and of itself, didn't heal her. She was a cripple in the pew who had learned how to settle for managing her mess. She had learned how to settle for just getting by.

Being a kingdom woman isn't summed up in just going to church more or doing more good things. It's about connecting with the One who gives hope.

Yet a kingdom woman never settles. I realize that what may have happened in your childhood or in your relationships—abuse or misuse—or even with your health or finances may have pushed you down. And the best you think you can ever reach is learning how to manage your pain. Maybe it looks unfixable and broken. After all, eighteen years is an awfully long time. But Jesus has more for your future than settling. Just like He had more for the woman who couldn't straighten up on her own:

> When Jesus saw her, he called her forward and said to her, "Woman, you are set free from your infirmity." Then he put his hands on her, and immediately she straightened up and praised God. (Verses 12–13)

She had been in church for a long time. Evidently you can go to church and not meet Jesus. You can be in the so-called right place and yet never run into Jesus. When she met Jesus, she met the One who was not going to do what had simply been done for eighteen years. Everyone else had dealt with the fruit, but Jesus went directly to the root.

Twice in the story of this woman, we are told the cause of her problem. She had been bound by Satan (verse 16). Her issue was not the issue. The issue went deeper than what she physically and emotionally faced.

See, that's important to know, because if the problem is caused by the Enemy, a doctor can't solve it. If Satan causes the problem, a sermon or a song can't solve it. Neither can it be solved by talking to friends, nor drowned by drinking too much, nor covered by retail therapy that you really can't afford. If the problem is spiritual in nature, then it needs a spiritual solution.

Keep in mind, I said it needs a spiritual solution, not a religious solution. There is a big difference between the two.

A key aspect of your life as a kingdom woman is in how you view and respond to Jesus. Is He merely something attached to a ritual or a routine—that of religion? Or do you view Him as a real Person who longs to have a relationship with you? The reason why so many people end up bound by issues is that they try to address the circumstances rather than appealing to the One who can address the root. The circumstances may be the result of a spiritual situation.

If something has gone on for that long, then you are dealing with the fruit and not the root. As long as Satan can keep you thinking about the fruit, he has hold of you. He doesn't mind if you go to your twelve-step program, talk to your friends all the time about it, or make New Year's resolutions time after time after time. He doesn't mind because he knows those are fruit-based solutions rather than root-based solutions.

If something in your life won't seem to lift no matter what you try or how you face it, I want you to look deeper than what you can see, because there is a spiritual root that needs to be addressed.

When Your Solution Comes Suddenly

The woman's solution came *suddenly*. Eighteen years of struggling to straighten up was healed *immediately*. See, with Jesus, it doesn't have to take a whole lot of time to change your view.

But I want you to notice that Jesus asked her to do something. He asked her to come to Him. She had to leave wherever she was standing and come over to Him. She had to make her way to Jesus, in faith, even though she couldn't stand up straight enough to see Him.

She couldn't quit or throw in the towel. She had to hold on to some hope even in what looked like a hopeless scenario. She couldn't say, "Well, I've come this far and that's as far as I'm going to go." Despite the aches that no doubt were common for her legs and back by then, despite the shame of being different from everyone else around her, she still went to Jesus.

For a kingdom woman to experience spiritual victory or relief from whatever may keep her head or heart down, she has to go to Jesus.

She didn't stop where she was. She placed her hope in His voice, and she kept going until she got to Him.

For a kingdom woman to experience spiritual victory or relief from whatever may keep her head or heart down, she has to go to Jesus. He is the only One who has authority over Satan and his minions. He is seated at the right hand of God in the heavenlies. That doesn't mean that Satan still can't disturb you, because he can. What that does mean is that Satan cannot disturb you when Jesus tells him to stop.

Jesus disarmed Satan when He died on the cross: "And having disarmed the powers and authorities, he made a public spectacle of them, triumphing over them by the cross" (Colossians 2:15). In other words, Jesus is the One calling the shots now. While Satan still has a great deal of power, Jesus has authority over Satan's power. If you want to get to the root of what has you discouraged and bent over, only Jesus holds the authority that you need to do so. If you are looking for your solutions in the physical realm when there is a spiritual cause, you are looking in the wrong location.

The Distraction Called Discouragement

One of the easiest ways to get a Christian off track from her personal destiny is through discouragement. I have seen this time and time again as I counsel people struggling with hopelessness. When you feel as if you have lost your hope—you are tired and want to give up—your head and your perspective only sees what's down. Your shoulders droop. And you forget that a future is out in front of you waiting to be grabbed.

The best thing that I can tell you to do if you are facing hopelessness is to listen to Jesus. Hear Him call your name. Like the woman who couldn't straighten up, don't quit. He doesn't want you to quit. He wants you to come closer to Him so He can put His hands on you and change your life *suddenly*.

If He doesn't answer your prayers right away, that's because He works healing in four ways. First, He can supernaturally heal you. Second, He can use human means to remedy your condition; third, He can give you strength to handle your condition until He corrects it. Fourth, He can enable you to persevere through the pain on earth until your full healing is made manifest in Heaven.

It's easy to want to give up; I understand that. The struggles you face are legitimate. If any of that sounds familiar, I want to encourage you to hang in there. A kingdom woman sets her eyes on Jesus, and He strengthens her to be all she was created to be.

Chrystal's Chronicles

I love to try new things, and I get excited fairly quickly when I am learning something new. Reminders are all over my home of things that I've set out to do but are incomplete.

Two years ago, I started a quilting class with my daughter. The quilt is in my closet folded up—about one-eighth of the way to completion.

I have started three scrapbooks: one for my son Jesse, one for my son Kanaan, and one for the family. None of them have more than six to eight pages.

I've started cleaning my closet more times than I can count. The back of the closet hasn't been touched for the last three years.

I have a pile of items to sell on craigslist or eBay. The pile is growing faster than the items sell.

Books are a passion of mine. However, I buy them faster than I can read them. Being less than ten minutes from a Barnes and Noble doesn't help my situation, and neither do my visits to the annual homeschool book fairs (yes, that's plural). Add to that the reading that I need to do to keep up with my children's learning.

I've started more Bible studies than I care to remember. The *Believing God* Bible study by Beth Moore is still on the bookshelf that it sat on when I started it two years ago. Both summers since, it's been on my to-do list.

Although I enjoy my life and never quite get stuck in a rut or fall into boredom often, I can't say that I finish as many things as I start.

And I have to admit that this ADD way of living isn't simply a result of a complex adult life or the by-product of motherhood-induced amnesia! Since my teenage years, I've often found myself so hyper-focused on one area of struggle that I just give up and yield to the temptation of throwing in the towel. Probably the best illustration of this was during my high school athletics.

When I was in high school, I ran track. Although my true desire was to be a sprinter and join the elite on the 400-meter relay team, the reality was I just wasn't fast enough. So I got put in longer distance races. Instead of being on the 400-meter relay team, I had to run the whole thing by myself. Needless to say, this was a struggle for me. The same folks who were running 100-meter dashes and could keep it up for a while were the same people who entered the 400-meter races. I ended up hopeless at many of the track meets as I settled into the idea of coming in toward the back of the pack.

Since I didn't seem wired for speed, I guess my coach figured I might be wired for endurance.

So my coach suggested I try the 800-meter race instead. She obviously thought I was a glutton for punishment. Since I didn't seem wired for speed, I guess my coach figured I might be wired for endurance.

I hated running this race. I think I might have preferred coming in last on a shorter race than placing higher running a race that required emotional and physical torture.

I hated feeling like my lungs were going to pop out of my chest cavity, and I hated the burning sensation of my soles over the spikes on the asphalt. My head hurt, my thighs ached, and my arms would be on fire. It was miserable. And that was when I was running the race at a track meet. Practices involved their own unique torture.

I had to run longer and faster in preparation for my performance at a meet. The 800-meter became two miles for practice in endurance, and 200-meter dashes expanded to eight 200-meter dashes in a row to develop speed. But I wanted to run. I struggled to do it well, but I wanted to do better, so I kept showing up even when I wanted to quit.

There is a story hidden in those years of running that illustrates a time when I wanted to quit like nothing else, but I didn't. It is a time when I had lost all hope but found a way to keep going.

We tell the story over and over at our family dinner table.

My dad came to watch me run the 800-meter race. I started out and established a good pace. I remember rounding the first curve and thinking that I felt full of energy and that my breathing had a good rhythm.

Even after the curve where I had the advantage of being in the inside lane, I was still in the lead. Now I started to get a bit excited. I remember hearing the pace of the girls behind me and thinking that I actually had a chance of placing.

When I went around the second curve, my adrenaline started flowing, and my heart pounded a bit faster. Surprisingly, I was still in control of my body, driving it forward with each step and each swing of the arms. I felt powerful.

On the second straightaway, words cannot express the pride that welled up in me as I heard my dad's voice in the stands, yelling, "Go, Chrystal, go, Chrystal! You can do it! Keep it up. Pace yourself . . . go . . . go . . . GO!"

Around the third curve, no one had passed me yet. There was a chance, a *real* chance, that I could take home a medal this time.

Yet before I knew it, that familiar feeling showed up. My lungs began to burn. My legs felt like lead. I willed my arms to pump faster, harder.

I was still in the lead.

But soon all of my power escaped through my nostrils; the capacity to control my breathing and my pace disappeared. My body and my flesh took over as I slowly realized that now even getting to the finish line might not happen.

In the distance, I could still hear my dad yelling "Chrystal, don't give up! Keep going. Come on . . . Come on . . . Keep running . . . Don't quit—you can do it!"

This time my appendages cared nothing for his words, and *they* were running the show.

I heard the steps of the girl closest to me increase a tad in speed. She saw the finish line approaching too, and she was definitely after me. Halfway up the straightaway, she passed me and took with her the last bit of resolve I owned. I had lost, and I heard the distant voice cry out in compassion for me.

"Awww, Chrystal!" my dad said. I knew what he meant by those words. I had given up.

A second set of feet closed in on me. When I say that I was barely walking at this point, that's *exactly* what I mean. Not only was I losing, but I wondered if I would even finish.

I attempted to set my eyes on the finish line, but it seemed too far away. I let my eyes fall to my feet instead. My head drooped. My once upright frame started to bend over.

Completing the last thirty feet to the finish line seemed to take three hours. Everything moved in slow motion. The voices from the crowd had become unintelligible. Except for one. I heard him, as loud as ever. He knew I was discouraged. He knew I had felt I had first place in the bag. He could tell by my posture that I had lost hope of even finishing now. But I heard him yell, "Go, Chrystal! You're almost there! Go! You can do it!"

When my right foot crossed the final white line, I came to a halt. I had finished! I hadn't given up! And I had grabbed the third place medal.

I truly feel that on that day (and every day my whole family laughs as my dad tells the story again), I was ready to quit. I simply stopped giving it my all when the first girl passed me. My flesh was weak, my spirit was faint, and I did not dig deep within to continue. At least not on my own.

I learned in that experience, though, that just as much as we need focus, diligence, and self-control to finish a race, sometimes we need someone encouraging us as well. Someone who believes that we can do it even when we have stopped believing in ourselves.

Our lives are not without mistakes. Every experience we have, God can use for His glory. He weaves our good and our not-so-good together to make a beautiful tapestry. But, oh, how I want to avoid unnecessary pitfalls by giving up way too soon.

I so yearn to be one of those people who goes the distance as a kingdom woman. I don't want my life only to leave loose threads, rough edges, or unfinished tasks. I want to finish, and I want to finish well. It makes me sad to think of times in the past when I haven't.

Just as much as we need focus, diligence, and self-control to finish a race, sometimes we need someone encouraging us as well.

When I look around at all of the projects and tasks that I have yet to complete, it makes me sad to think that I will fall prey to every distracting activity that comes my way rather than keeping first things first.

What can I do? How can I change?

Hebrews 12:1 tells us, "Therefore, since we are surrounded by such a great cloud of witnesses, let us throw off everything that hinders and the sin that so easily entangles, and let us *run* with perseverance the *race* marked out for us."

How do I know which race is mine? Only God can tell me. How can I get this information from God? I have to spend time with Him. I have to view Him as more than religion or a system of rights and wrongs. Jesus is real. The relationship that He longs to have with me is real. And only He can help me lift my head up when the tiredness from life causes me to cave in. Only His voice matters when I'm ready to give up.

My dad makes an interesting point when he teaches on Hebrews 12:1. The verse doesn't tell us to throw off the sins (plural) that hinder us and entangle us. It says to throw off *the sin* (singular). We aren't to get weighed down trying to fix this, that, and the other. Because if we don't get the main thing right, we'll never get the rest to fall in line. The sin that this verse refers to is the sin of unbelief, a lack of faith. When Jesus told the woman who couldn't straighten up that He wanted her to come to Him, she could have said no. She could have said that she'd tried church already. She could have said that she was tired. She could have said that her back hurt. She could have said that she didn't want to be disappointed again—so why try. Instead, she demonstrated faith despite a lifetime of hopelessness.

Life is hard. Life is tough. Life is *real*. But on the day when I ran that 800-meter race, others ran too. The race was difficult for everyone. My legs weren't the only ones burning. My lungs weren't the only ones heaving. My thighs weren't the only ones that felt lifeless and heavy. But the good thing is that we all finished.

I don't think I'm a quitter by nature. However, I do get easily distracted. Isn't that just like Satan, though? If he can't convince us to quit, he just keeps us distracted.

Sisters, we are each running a race, and Jesus is calling each of us to run with Him, to keep from being distracted, and to live with purpose. He doesn't want us to run with our heads down any longer. He wants us to fix our eyes on Him, to straighten up and let His voice push us on. Can you hear Him? He's calling your name. He's cheering for you, telling you that you can make it and encouraging you as you run your race. You don't need to give up. You don't have to drop your gaze toward your feet.

We serve a God who knows that we get tired. He is the same God who spent time on this earth, clothed in flesh, running His own race, catching His breath, and enduring physical, emotional, and mental fatigue and pain. But be encouraged. Our God not only can identify with us as we run, but, if we will receive it, He also offers power and strength so that we can run our own race well.

Stand Tall

I'll always remember that day cheering on Chrystal as she ran. Her story reminds us that even though life gets hard, we have Someone on our side. He is asking each of us to keep going and not quit. Jesus' death on the cross won your victory in everything. He didn't just die so that you would be able to manage your mess or misery. He died so that you might have life and have it abundantly.

One final thought from the story of the woman who couldn't straighten up is found in Luke 13:16, where Jesus gives us a key insight into the rights of a kingdom woman: "This woman, *a daughter of Abraham . . .*" Did you catch that? The woman Jesus healed was a daughter of Abraham. God had made a covenant with Abraham all the way back in time, as recorded in Genesis, that He would bless Abraham and his descendants. What God promised to give to Abraham held true for Abraham's children as well.

This woman was connected to Abraham, so she was connected to his covenantal promises. She had a right to be blessed. The same is true for you. As a believer in Jesus Christ, you are a child of Abraham (Galatians 3:29) and, therefore, have rights given to you by the covenant. As a kingdom woman, you have a right to fully experience your destiny. You do not have to live doomed to disappointment or hopelessness.

You can stand tall and walk straight.

> *As a kingdom woman, you have a right to fully experience your destiny. You do not have to live doomed to disappointment.*

3

A WOMAN OF EXCELLENCE

Most of us prefer excellence. We may not state it openly, but our actions reveal it. For example, we want excellence in the medical care that we receive. We don't want to hear a doctor say he doesn't really know what's wrong with us but would like to operate on us to find out what's wrong. When it comes to our physical well-being, we want a doctor who knows what he or she is doing. We want excellence.

When we go to a restaurant, we don't want our food just thrown together. We want it prepared with excellence. We don't want our server smacking on gum while tossing our food just anywhere on our table. We want excellence.

We certainly don't want to fly on an airplane that hasn't been excellently crafted. We don't want the captain to come on the loudspeaker before takeoff talking about how they taped portions of the wing together. That would be unnerving, and most people, if not all, would quickly disembark. When we fly, we want excellence.

When we spend money to buy a car, we want excellent craftsmanship. We don't want to be driving it into the repair shop week after week as piece after piece on our new vehicle breaks. We want excellence.

Even though we want excellence in the things that we receive, often we lack excellence in the things that we do. Yet a kingdom woman understands that her unique position calls her to a higher standard than what the culture has set. She knows that God has ordained her for a destiny of excellence.

Being a woman of excellence simply means living your finest, giving your best. When we stand before God at the judgment seat of Christ, He will specifically be looking for excellence. We read about this in Paul's letter to the church at Corinth:

> Every man's work shall be made manifest: for the day shall declare it,
> because it shall be revealed by fire; and the fire shall try every man's work
> of what sort it is. (1 Corinthians 3:13, KJV)

When one day you stand before God, He will not only ask how much you did for Him but will also judge how excellent it was. Did you merely give God your leftovers, or was quality attached to your life even in the mundane tasks that pile up in a woman's life? Because your days are often filled with things that others may not see—things that have to get done that you may never hear gratitude for or that may not be on display. It is easy to pull back on the quality of what you do. Yet God wants you to rise to a higher standard. He desires excellence in all you do. And your excellence will not go unnoticed.

God wants you to rise to a higher standard. He desires excellence in all you do.

In the biblical story of Ruth, Ruth had what would be considered a mundane and overlooked job. She had traveled with her mother-in-law to a new land. Having been widowed, she did not have money or property. To simply get by in life, she had to carry out the task of gleaning. She had to gather the leftovers from the farmers in the field after they had reaped the harvest. Ruth probably never thought that anyone would ever judge how well she did that job, but she did it with excellence. And because she did—all of her life showed excellence—she was later rewarded as she became the wife of a man named Boaz and then the great-grandmother of King David of Israel, ultimately one of the direct ancestors of our eternal King Jesus Christ.

The following passage reveals Ruth's character:

> "The Lord bless you, my daughter," [Boaz] replied. "This kindness is
> greater than that which you showed earlier: You have not run after the

younger men, whether rich or poor. And now, my daughter, don't be afraid. I will do for you all you ask. All my fellow townsmen know that you are a *woman of noble character*." (Ruth 3:10–11)

Ruth's reputation spoke volumes about her character and destiny. She was a woman of excellence in her decisions and actions. As a result, God lifted her from a low position and situated her in a life of honor.

Excellence is a spiritual issue. It differs from success because success generally has to do with how much money you make, what job you have, or how much prestige you receive. Success has to do with reaching a level that the world recognizes as successful. While success belongs to a few, excellence is available to all.

Excellence is not concerned with how you compare to others. Excellence is concerned with how you are compared to the potential of how you are supposed to be. In other words, excellence has to do with God's destiny for you. Are you progressively pressing forward and moving toward what He wants for you? Are you defining your decisions, thoughts, and actions by the highest quality and authenticity you have to offer? That is the measure of true excellence.

God has called you, like Ruth, to be a woman of excellence. You may not think that anyone is watching you or that what you are doing carries much significance based on the culture's values. Yet in some obscure field while collecting remnants of other people's meals, Ruth gained a reputation of excellence. God saw her, and He was pleased with what He saw. He granted her favor in the eyes of all who saw her as well.

Paul tells us that all of our lives should be marked with excellence:

Finally, brothers, we *instructed* you how to live in order to please God, as in fact you are living. Now we ask you and urge you in the Lord Jesus to do this more and more. (1 Thessalonians 4:1)

Excellence should be your aim as a kingdom woman. Proverbs reminds us that the excellent woman, or excellent wife, is a rare treasure of the highest value: "An excellent wife who can find? She is far more precious than jewels" (31:10, ESV).

God's excellence is to serve as your model—"Sing unto the LORD; for he hath done excellent things" (Isaiah 12:5, KJV). Excellence is the standard for which you ought to aim, since you are a child made in His image.

> Excellence *doesn't mean* perfection. *It means doing all you can with all you have at that moment.*

Keep in mind that *excellence* doesn't mean *perfection*. It means doing all you can with all you have at that moment. I'll never forget when Chrystal ran that 800-meter race. I couldn't have been more proud of her. She had started out so quickly that I knew it was likely she would run out of momentum before reaching the finish line. But I admired her tenacity and her zeal, and she learned an important lesson about pacing herself as well as one on the value of finishing. The thing I was proud of the most was that when she saw the other two runners pass her by, and as her body screamed out to her to quit, she didn't. She kept going. She didn't let the reality of her past—the good (being so far in front at the beginning) or the bad (having two runners pass her)—affect her present. She focused on where she was at that very moment.

Paul penned one of the greatest passages in Scripture about pressing forward despite setbacks or discouragement. Paul, a leader in the Christian faith, spoke of his own faith journey when he wrote the following:

> Not that I have already obtained all this, or have already been made perfect, but I *press on* to take hold of that for which Christ Jesus took hold of me. . . . Forgetting what is behind and straining toward what is ahead, I *press on* toward the goal to win the prize for which God has called me heavenward in Christ Jesus. (Philippians 3:12–14)

Here is the secret to your life as a kingdom woman of excellence: a short memory coupled with a clear direction. If you are going to live in excellence, you have to forget yesterday. Whether it was good, bad, or ugly, if it's yesterday, you need to let it go. When you carry yesterday further than you ought to, you ruin today. If you ruin today, then you spoil tomorrow.

If anyone should have been held hostage by yesterday, it would have been Ruth. She knew what it was like to be young and married, with plenty of food, and to live in a culture that understood and accepted her. She also knew what it was like to lose her husband and leave her homeland with nothing to her name. But if Ruth had continually wallowed in both the good and the bad of her yesterday, she wouldn't have had any mind left to be excellent in her today.

Ruth was a woman of excellence because she was not held hostage to yesterday. She knew how to press on.

You are to learn from yesterday, but don't live in it. The way to get yesterday out of today is to do what Paul said—to have a tomorrow focus: "Forgetting what is behind and straining toward what is ahead, I *press on . . .*"

When you see something in your rearview mirror that catches your attention as you are driving, it slows you down. Your attention is now focused on what is behind you rather than on what is up ahead. As a result, you lift your foot off the accelerator and slow down. Yet when you set your focus on what is ahead of you, you are able to keep your foot steady on the accelerator and move forward. As you do, what is behind you gets smaller and smaller until it eventually fades away. You don't get rid of yesterday by talking about it all of the time; you get rid of its effect on you by moving forward.

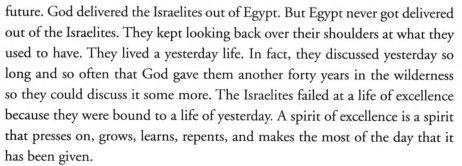

You don't get rid of yesterday by talking about it all of the time; you get rid of its effect on you by moving forward.

God told Israel that He had a future for them, and it was a good future flowing with milk and honey, meaning it was an abundant future. God delivered the Israelites out of Egypt. But Egypt never got delivered out of the Israelites. They kept looking back over their shoulders at what they used to have. They lived a yesterday life. In fact, they discussed yesterday so long and so often that God gave them another forty years in the wilderness so they could discuss it some more. The Israelites failed at a life of excellence because they were bound to a life of yesterday. A spirit of excellence is a spirit that presses on, grows, learns, repents, and makes the most of the day that it has been given.

An Example of an Excellent Woman

Another problem that often stands in the way of a life of excellence comes when we live for people more than for God. We make people our standard rather than God. We do our job for those around us, we work for our family's praise, we make our actions and choices in light of how people are going to respond to us rather than whether God is going to say that we are excellent. It's easy for us to look at only what we can see, but God sees all. He even sees the most mundane tasks that no one else might ever notice. Martin Luther supposedly said, "[Even] a dairy maid can milk cows to the glory of God." Paul wrote, "So whether you eat or drink or whatever you do, do it all for the glory of God" (1 Corinthians 10:31).

Dwell on excellence. Don't think of what you can do to get by. Don't allow yourself to think sloppy thoughts. Think about whether God is applauding all that you do. Think of yourself the way He views you, as a woman destined for excellence.

Excellent people who set their minds on God don't have to be prodded to do well. They fulfill their responsibilities willingly because they do them unto the Lord.

Again, excellence is not perfection. Rather, it defines your movement. Are you moving forward? Are you progressing to be more and more like Jesus Christ? Are you investing in the moment rather than being bound by yesterday or worrying about tomorrow? Excellence means going to the next level. It shows up in little ways more than it does in big ways. It is a pattern, a lifestyle.

Paul gets a bad rap sometimes from women. He didn't mince words, and he didn't make a lot of friends with his writings about women. But one of the greatest honors he ever gave in his writings was given to a woman of excellence. In the last chapter of his hallmark work, the book of Romans, Paul wrapped up his thoughts. As he did, he sent his greetings and well-wishes for those whom he loved. He had just finished his concluding statement when he wrote, "The God of peace be with you all. Amen" (15:33).

His very next statement, as he began his farewell greetings, focused on a kingdom woman named Phoebe. There are only two verses on Phoebe in the Bible, but they speak volumes about her excellence. Phoebe isn't hidden somewhere down in the midst of a litany of names. Paul began by expressly highlighting this woman:

> I commend to you our sister Phoebe, a servant of the church in Cenchrea. I ask you to receive her in the Lord in a way worthy of the saints and to give her any help she may need from you, for she has been a great help to many people, including me. (16:1–2)

Phoebe's excellence, like Ruth's excellence and like the excellence of the Proverbs 31 woman, is to be your excellence as well. It is your highest calling as a kingdom woman, because through a life of excellence, you bring glory to God. Excellent people who set their minds on God don't have to be prodded to do well. They fulfill their responsibilities willingly because they do them unto the Lord.

Chrystal's Chronicles

Not too long ago, it occurred to me as I got up to clean the kitchen for the umpteenth time, that I didn't feel like it. What else I realized was how many times over the last weeks, months, and years I've felt the same way about quite a few of my responsibilities in motherhood.

The truth is, there is very little room for selfishness in this place of servanthood. If I took the route of bemoaning my fate, things would only get worse, and then I'd have a bigger hole of self-pity to dig myself out of. If I don't do the dishes, they pile up. If I don't do the laundry, we have no clean clothes. If I don't pay the bills, we have no electricity.

I can't even imagine what life would look like around here if I did only what I felt like doing. So I've discovered that this path of being a kingdom woman is not a path for sissies or for women who are not made of tough stuff.

I've discovered that my best days are the ones when I arise early to get myself together before the troops converge, and when I go to bed later than everyone else to make sure that things are at a good starting place for tomorrow. Believe me, I do not prefer to wake first and sleep last. However, it seems to be the key to having a smooth day.

Today, for example, I began cooking dinner shortly after finishing breakfast. Putting a chicken in the Crock-Pot made my dinner prep all of thirty minutes at 6:00 PM. Making gravy, roasting potatoes, cooking rice, and throwing together a salad was almost effortless. I also made a menu for the rest of the week, which allowed me to make my grocery list, which made it possible to get in and out of the grocery store in thirty minutes. Being semi-dressed (dressed but not glamorous) before my crew arose allowed me to be somewhat composed when my doorbell rang.

Deciding to take my home and family on like a kingdom woman and not cowering under the weight of the tedious and mundane make the flow of my day so much easier.

These are small things in which I strive for excellence, and yet they are huge in return when I can sigh at the end of the day because I realize that I've given my all.

A day like today shines in comparison to other days when I have been down, behind, hungry, discombobulated, and stressed. Most of those times involve my indulgent self-pity about how hard things are as a woman pulled in so many directions and needed by so many people.

Deciding to take my home and family on like a kingdom woman and not cowering under the weight of the tedious and mundane make the flow of my day so much easier.

If I stare back in time too long, I'll find things that I wish I had done better or cringe at all of the things I opted not to do at all. Looking in the rearview mirror of yesterday, I see lots of "would haves," "could haves," and "should haves." But those years are spent. They are gone. How I used that time is how I used it, and I can't go back.

But I can take a step forward into a brighter tomorrow.

Each day I am blessed to live gives me another day to press on and do the best I can with what I have. It gives me another day to live as a woman of excellence. No, most people will never know how many loads of laundry I do in a year, how many spills I clean up, or how many homeschool lessons I prepare and grade. But God knows. He knows my every move, and He has created me to make my every move in a spirit that is nothing less than excellent. He knows the same about you, too.

Often, the life of a woman—young or old, married or single, presents opportunities to perform thankless jobs in many ways. The temptation is there to pull back or just get by. But when I start to think that way, I remember my aunt and the example she has always lived in excellence. Never married, she dedicated herself solely to the Lord and has given herself to be "Auntie" to her nieces and nephews and now her great-nieces and great-nephews in so many ways. She also dedicated herself to starting and running the children's program at our church for decades—while simultaneously getting her PhD. She is a woman of excellence, and when asked what motivates her to be that way, she will reply, "Because of that day."

"That day" is her reference to the day that she expects to stand before Jesus and the day He will test the quality of her work. The truth is that we all will face "that day," and if the service we have offered Him is excellent, we will hear those blessed words, "Well done, good and faithful servant. . . . Enter into the joy of your master" (Matthew 25:23, ESV).

I want to hear those words. I want what I do and what I have done to make Jesus smile on that day. A life of excellence isn't easy. There aren't always accolades, especially when you choose to make important the things that are important to the Lord. But there will be one very meaningful accolade on "that day."

Where does the Lord prick your heart to do more, go further, or raise the bar? While my challenge is in the grind of motherhood, it is not the only place where excellence in womanhood is required. On your job, are you content to keep the status quo or do you go the extra mile in your daily responsibilities? In your appearance, are you satisfied with the way you are, or are you aiming to be healthier? Do you do the best you can with what you have to represent your Savior when you step out the door? What about your marriage? Are you settling for a comfortable coexistence with your husband, or do you put your best foot forward in an effort to have a heavenly marriage here on earth? If you desire marriage and are waiting on God to answer the desire of your heart, what are you doing with your time? Are you using your time for His glory, or are you merely marking time or wondering how much longer your biological clock will tick? While you wait on a mate, are you seizing every opportunity God brings to use your time, talents, and resources to further the kingdom? That question is not just for the single woman; it is for the retired woman, the content woman, or the woman who feels that she has arrived.

"But we all, with open face beholding as in a glass the glory of the Lord, are changed into the same image from glory to glory, even as by the Spirit of the Lord" (2 Corinthians 3:18, KJV). Excellence on earth is not a destination; it is a continual process of transformation into who God wants us to be. The excellence He desires from us is not a level of superiority or distinction that we can achieve on our own either. Our treasure is not in our "earthen vessels," but it is in the excellence of His power in us (2 Corinthians 4:7, KJV).

> *Excellence is not a destination; it is a continual process of transformation into who God wants us to be.*

Excellent is what we will be when we are made perfect in the next life. However, in the meantime, our job is to strive for the excellence the Father has revealed to us in the season of life that we are in, in the context of our lives right now. And as we commit to pursue this life, the life of an excellent woman, the Father transforms us into the likeness of His Son.

Psalm 16:11 says, "You have made known to me the path of life; you will fill me with joy in your presence, with eternal pleasures at your right hand." Choosing excellence now is to choose the fruit of joy and pleasure in days to come.

When we choose excellence, God gets the glory.

When we choose excellence, we benefit from walking in the fullness of His joy on earth and investing in the pleasures of eternity in heaven.

So, my friend, choose the excellent way. And do so not for the reasons that you can see but for the things which are not seen and that are eternal (2 Corinthians 4:18).

Full Destiny

To be excellent is to be more than just one of the crowd. It is to live in a way that sets you apart as special and unique. Just as Chrystal said and Phoebe lived her life, what you do and how you do it draws the attention of others to the glory of God. Like Ruth, it positions you into the fullest manifestation of your destiny. You'll never be excellent if you make the world your standard. A kingdom woman knows her true value and shows the reflection of how God sees her. She makes God's standard her own in all that she does.

Think about it in terms of one of the least-thanked groups in our society: the trash collectors. It's not what you would call a high-class job. However, in New York back in 1990 and again in 2006, the trash collectors went on strike.[1] All of a sudden, these typically overlooked and unseen individuals became the most significant people in the city because the whole city realized how much it needed them.

As a kingdom woman, you have been uniquely designed to fulfill a life of excellence.

Much of what comes in the life of a kingdom woman will not make the headlines. For much of what you do, you may never receive thanks. People may only notice when you are not there or you don't do it. But that reality doesn't change your significance. You are a rare find, a precious jewel. As a kingdom woman, you have the virtue of excellence, and although you may not hear it as much as you want, or even as much as you should, those around you need you.

Your family needs you.

Your church needs you.

Your community needs you.

In fact, the world needs you. As a kingdom woman, you have been uniquely designed to fulfill a life of excellence.

4

A Woman
of Commitment

Some people have suggested that history would have been considerably different if the three wise men had actually been three wise women. Since that's not what happened, the best we can do is conjecture what might have occurred if three wise women welcomed the baby Jesus rather than the three wise men.

If it had been the *wise women* rather than the *wise men*, some say that the wise women would have asked for directions, arrived on time, helped deliver the baby, cleaned the stable, made a casserole, and brought practical gifts from Babies"R"Us—including diapers, wipes, bibs, and formula.

There is no doubt that women, as a gender, are greatly gifted. Multitasking to a woman often comes as easy as solo-tasking to a man. Research shows us that women are often more spiritually inclined than men as well. According to the Pew Research Center's Forum on Religion and Public Life in its analysis of the US Religious Landscape Survey, women are

- more likely than men to be affiliated with a religion,
- more likely than men to pray daily,
- more likely than men to believe in God, and
- more likely than men to regularly attend worship services.[1]

Women seem to have it together, making the most of their days and the gifts God has given to them. Yet even though women are frequently skilled in the art of managing life situations and achieving results, sometimes the challenges can be too much. That's true for anyone. Life can throw curve balls.

Or maybe it's not a curve ball at all. Maybe it's just that life keeps throwing fastballs—one after another. And the challenges start to pile up on top of each other, making it easy to feel that you will never be free from the stress, pain, or emptiness that can occur when you have depleted all of your natural resources while trying to manage each and every thing.

When this happens, it is easy to want to throw in the towel. But others' lives depend on the functioning and well-being of a woman who is juggling so much. Even if you throw in the towel, life still keeps throwing challenges at you. You have to address the trials.

A Woman Who Didn't Throw in the Towel

The next woman I want to look at was a capable woman who may have thought she had it good at one point. This woman's saga shows up in the Old Testament. Now, I realize that the Old Testament may seem distant from the situations of today, but what was recorded in this part of the Bible is for our benefit: "Now these things happened to them as an example, but they were written down for our instruction" (1 Corinthians 10:11, ESV). The Old Testament is a relevant book even though the stories may seem out of date to our contemporary world. The Bible stories offer us principles that transcend time—spiritual principles to guide our lives even today.

> *The Bible stories offer us principles that transcend time—spiritual principles to guide our lives even today.*

The kingdom woman I want us to look at is in 2 Kings 4. While we don't know much about her, we do know she was wise, because when she found herself in a predicament beyond her own abilities to solve, she sought out the local prophet.

We also know that this woman had been married. To be married during biblical times was a source not only of security but also of dignity. In addition to that, she had been fruitful. Scripture tells us that this woman had children. She had been blessed by the best.

Then out of the blue, her life was turned upside down. Her husband died. She lost the steady income that he had provided, so she tried to find a way to feed and clothe her children on her own, but soon the debts began to pile up. When the debts piled up, as was the custom in her culture, the creditors then had a right to come seize her two children to have them work as slaves to pay off what she owed.

There is probably no greater pain that a woman can feel than seeing someone mess with her children and not being able to protect or shield them. I can't imagine the grief in this woman's heart as she thought about her precious two children soon being used, misused, and most likely abused as slaves. That will bring out the mama bear in any kingdom woman, for sure.

We are looking at a woman who was dealing with several layers of pain all at the same time. No doubt she experienced emotional pain because of the loss of her husband and the fear of losing her children. She had now become a suffering single parent.

In addition to that, she experienced financial pain. "The creditor has come to take my two children to be his slaves" (2 Kings 4:1, ESV). The bills kept piling up while the creditors kept calling. She had no husband or money and was about to lose her children. For anyone, that would be too much to handle.

To add insult to injury, she was also in physical pain. She was hungry. "Your servant has nothing in the house except a jar of oil" (verse 4:2). If all she had was a jar of oil, then she definitely didn't have any food. Have you ever been hungry? It is less likely in our country to find someone who truly knows what it means to be hungry. But still today around the world, people go to bed completely hungry.

Even in this woman's emotional, financial, and physical pain, she faced an ever-greater pain. She was in spiritual pain. She revealed something important about her deceased husband: "Your servant my husband is dead, and you know that your servant *feared the LORD*" (verse 4:1). Nothing is worse than fearing God and yet not being able to locate Him when you need Him the most. That is true spiritual suffering.

Her husband had feared the Lord, and they had been a God-fearing family. Not only had God allowed her husband's life to end, but now this woman was at risk of losing her children as well. I would not be surprised if doubts ran across her mind, questioning God. If this is what living a God-fearing life gets you, then why do it?

If I took a poll right now of everyone reading this book, how many of you would say you know what it is like to be in spiritual pain? You know what it is like for life's situations to not add up. You know what it is like to feel as though the God who says He will never leave you or forsake you doesn't seem to be around.

You've been serving Him, obeying Him, seeking Him, giving to Him, worshipping Him, and helping those He loves. You've been doing the *do* of the Christian life. And it's likely that you've been doing it from a sincere heart. Yet you can't pay the bills. You feel alone. You are hurting. And what's worse, you can't seem to find God anywhere.

Maybe you can't identify with every pain that the woman in 2 Kings 4 faced, but my guess is that you can identify with one. I've counseled way too many people over nearly forty years of ministry to not acknowledge that this is often a common thread in the lives of those who are hurting. The question I've heard a lot is "Where is God when I need Him most?"

> *When God is silent, He is not still. God does some of His best work in the dark.*

My reply is always the same: When God is silent, He is not still. God does some of His best work in the dark. He does some of His best work when you don't think He's doing a thing. He's behind the scenes, working it out. He is faithful even though you feel you cannot see Him.

He has a plan for you, and it is a good one. Your commitment in the dark is the path to your victory in the light. Commitment to keeping your faith, seeking God, and not throwing in the towel when no human solution is in sight is the secret to exchanging emptiness for abundance.

The Prophet and the Plan

A prophet in the Bible was someone who spoke on behalf of God. A prophet was God's voice to humanity. His duty was to say what God was saying. He was not simply a teacher. A teacher can take God's Word and say, "This is what God means," as he explains God's truth. But a prophet was more than a teacher because a prophet would not only be able to say, "This is what God means," but would also be able to apply the words of God to a specific situation. A prophet could tell you what God was saying as it related directly to you. It was not the Word of God in abstract form. Rather, it was the Word of God for a unique scenario or need. When a prophet spoke to someone specifically, it was God's Word with that person's name written right on it.

Have you ever been to a church service when it seemed like what the preacher was teaching could have had your name written all over it? You felt like no one else was even in the room; the message was directly aimed and spoken just for you. That is when the Holy Spirit has taken God's Word and turned it into a prophetic word for your situation.

Why did the woman in 2 Kings 4 go to the prophet? She went to him because she was in a situation that only God could fix. Have you ever been in a situation that only God can fix? You've tried everything that you can think of to fix it, but nothing has worked.

If you are in or have been in a situation like that, it is most likely that God has you exactly where He wants you. Sometimes God lets you be in a situation that only He can fix, so you will discover that He is the One who can fix it.

You will never discover that God is all you need until you get to the place where God is all you have. When you've been reduced beyond your own abilities to make things work. When the bank won't give you the loan. When your friends won't answer the phone. When you've talked to every person you can think of, and no one is intervening on your behalf. When the doctors can't pinpoint what is ailing you. You are in a situation that is beyond you and even beyond those who are around you. That is where this woman in the Bible was, so she went straight to the prophet.

She needed a word just for her. She didn't need a sermon, a Bible study, or

> *Sometimes God lets you be in a situation that only He can fix, so you will discover that He is the One who can fix it.*

a song. She needed a *rhema*—a word with her name on it. In Scripture, God communicates different ways. A *logos* is a general word to all believers.[2] Yet a *rhema* is a specific utterance with a specific situation or person in mind. This woman went to the prophet because she needed a word just for her situation, a *rhema*.[3]

The prophet replied with a *rhema* just for her; however, when he did, he raised an interesting question. He didn't answer the way it seemed like he should answer. Instead, he asked a question of his own, "What shall I do for you? Tell me; what have you in the house?" (2 Kings 4:2, ESV). It's an odd question. In fact, it's a question on top of a question. First, Elisha asked, "What shall I do for you?" But he didn't give her enough time to answer before he asked, "What have you in the house?"

The first question became even more critical in its meaning once he followed it up with the second question. The prophet was making it known that in coming to him, the woman wasn't going to get an ordinary answer. The key word in the first question is *I*. In referring to himself, he set up his next question.

His next question did not consist of polite words. By asking it, he let the widow know that by coming to him, she shouldn't expect what everyone else would offer as solutions. He was not going to do what her friends, family, or neighbors would have tried to do.

Instead, Elisha brought up what could look like another problem in and of itself. He highlighted her insufficiency by asking what she had in her home. The woman didn't deflect the odd question. She knew that his reply wasn't going to consist of the expected. So she replied frankly, "Your servant has *nothing* in the house except *a jar of oil.*"

"Exactly," Elisha responded (in a loose translation). Then he proceeded to tell her just what he wanted her to do with that "nothing" plus one "jar of oil."

> Go around and ask all your neighbors for empty jars. Don't ask for just a
> few. Then go inside and shut the door behind you and your sons. Pour oil
> into all the jars, and as each is filled, put it to one side. (Verses 3–4)

Not only did Elisha want her to experience her own nothingness, but he also specifically told her to go gather from her neighbors their "empty jars" as well. He didn't tell her to go collect their oil. He told her to collect their "nothing" too. In doing so, he essentially increased the volume of her emptiness by magnifying it.

I don't know about you, but to me that sounds like a crazy bit of advice. The widow told the prophet that she had nothing in her house, and he told her to go collect everyone else's nothingness as well. Going from bad to worse, he then told her that after she collected her neighbors' empty pots, pans, and buckets, she was to take her one measly jar of oil and fill up their jars with her own. She was to pour what little oil she had out of her one jar and put it into someone else's. The request was illogical at best and insane at worst.

But he was the prophet, and he had given a *rhema* from the Lord to the widow. It was up to her to decide whether she was going to commit to his instructions in faith or abandon the mission altogether. After all, he didn't give her a solution that she could follow partially. Once she stepped out her door; walked the dirt path over to her first neighbor's home; entered her neighbor's dwelling; asked for pots, pans, and buckets; and stacked them all to carry them back home, word would be out about what she was doing. Either she needed to follow his instructions through to completion or she would be a laughing stock to those in her neighborhood as well as a disappointment to the prophet.

Keep in mind that faith doesn't always make sense. But it does make miracles.

Yet because the widow committed herself to the instructions of the prophet, she experienced a miracle. Kingdom women obey God's Word even when it seems to make no sense. Keep in mind that faith doesn't always make sense. But it does make miracles.

Chrystal's Chronicles

While washing dishes after a family meal, I began contemplating the value of the pots and pans that I have. I remembered back to when I got married and received various pots and pans as wedding gifts. Each time I would cook, I would furiously wash them afterward to try to keep them looking new and unused. You can guess that my obsession with clean pots and pans didn't last too long, as more cooking blemishes appeared faster than I could clean them.

Growing up, I couldn't understand why my mother let her pots look "messy." Now, as a grown woman myself, I know why. Good cooks have seasoned pots and pans. My mother's favorite pans were usually the ugliest. My grandmother's all-purpose skillet was cast-iron—a veteran of many years. My Crock-Pot is priceless, but it has scuff marks of its own. If a pot or pan isn't marked up, then that would indicate that it hasn't been used.

We tend to look at people who have life wounds and wonder what has happened to them. Sometimes those battle scars are a result of struggles that person brought on herself. Sometimes that person may have had no fault at all in the acquisition of her injuries. From the outside looking in, we may stop and stare because we tend to dislike noticeable imperfections. The fact of the matter is that many women with scuff marks are simply seasoned and, therefore, more available for God's use because of their imperfection, inadequacy, or emptiness.

Like the widow who was down to her last jar of oil, many women know what it is like to be down to their last handful of energy, money, hope, or joy and still hear God's voice asking them to give it all to Him by giving it all to others.

I can't imagine giving up my last bit of food and putting it into other people's jars. But sometimes the things that God asks us to do seem just as strange and far-fetched. Yet when we do them, we get to see Him show up in a way we would never expect. Granted, we are sometimes worse for the wear, externally—a little tried, tested, and bruised—but so are some of the most treasured pots and pans in our kitchens.

Living without smudges is possible, I suppose, but I don't think that's what God looks for when He searches for a heart that will commit to follow Him. Instead, He looks for whether the woman has learned to depend on Him, whether she knows the value of commitment and the supreme power of faith. That's what He looked for when He sent the prophet to help the widow who was struggling just to survive with her two children, and that's what He still looks for today.

One of the surest ways to stay off God's miracle radar is to stay put in the cabinet of life in order to keep looking shiny and new. God isn't looking for shiny and new; He is looking for a seasoned faith.

Just like my pots and pans, we have to count the cost of living as kingdom women. A kingdom woman realizes that sometimes the stove God places her upon will get really hot. A kingdom woman understands that, at times, the stuff of life that she is required to "cook" may be very messy and leave evidence of her participation. But are we going to experience the good with the bad? Or are we going to experience nothing at all, hidden safely away in a cabinet?

As I grow older—the correct cooking term would be *seasoned*—I'm learning to fear the elements less. I'm learning that it is more valuable to step out in faith for God to use me than to hide away somewhere in my Christian walk where I won't risk a bump or a bruise. I'm learning that to walk with a bit of life's mess still on me—a few smudges, scars, or nicks—is a testimony to a God who, despite what little I have to offer Him and how insignificant it may seem in the big scheme of life, looks at more than what the world sees.

He looks at my heart. He looks at whether I respond to Him, like the widow, with faith and trust, or whether I judge my neighbors' emptiness or my own. When we come in faith before a supreme and powerful God, He can make something out of nothing. Not only can He meet my needs, but He can also use me to meet other people's needs as well.

The world we live in does not treasure bruises and brokenness, inadequacy or empty hands. The world despises weakness and the idea of a willingly submissive soul. The world does not value what God values—humility, emptiness, meekness, and the beauty of a servant's heart. Our world does not appreciate or esteem difficulty, tough times, and the stuff of life that leaves a residue of grit or grime.

But God does.

God loves people, women, who are willing to trade in their shining exteriors for usefulness in His kingdom. God treasures the one who desires His purposes over an easy life. Our Father values women who love His plan for them more than they love their plan for themselves—even

> *God treasures the one who desires His purposes over an easy life.*

when His plan may hurt. God loves the woman who trusts that He will only let her experience the grit and grime necessary for Him to fully use her for His glory.

God loves a seasoned sister—a kingdom woman who chooses to be filled with His love and power—whether or not she has any of her own to draw from.

The Path of Wisdom

One of the biggest challenges in our Christian experience is committing to follow God's wisdom rather than the world's. The world's wisdom is sometimes referred to as worldliness. Worldliness is simply that system set up by Satan that seeks to leave God out.

When the widow approached the prophet, he made perfectly clear from the very start that God's way was going to be different from anyone else's. God's way often includes paths that we cannot figure out and that don't make sense. If the woman was down to her last jar of oil, why was he telling her to go get everyone else's empty jars as well? Yet that is exactly what the prophet did. He expanded the view of the woman beyond herself. In gathering everyone else's jars, she now saw not only her own needs but theirs as well. Not only that, but the prophet also laid out a path of commitment to her that would demonstrate her faith.

The reason why so many people today are living short of the victorious kingdom life is because they have settled for conversion. Conversion is great—it reconciles you to God's kingdom for eternity. But for God's kingdom power to be active in you requires commitment. That requires dedication to His Word and His way. If there is no commitment to the King and His kingdom, and you choose to follow the world's definition of wisdom or solutions instead, you will not see the manifestation of the King, because Jesus clearly stated, "My kingdom is not of this world" (John 18:36).

When you come to Jesus with your challenges, like the prophet He says, "What shall *I* do for you?" This is a reminder that the One you approached is going to have a different path that requires commitment in order to see the miracle from it. There are four principles that I want to look at from the widow's path of commitment.

The first principle learned is that God's way is the best way to address life's problems. The widow's problem did not get solved until she got a prophetic word from God through Elijah. Until then, she was stuck. She was stuck with only human opinion. Human opinion is a lot like junk food. If you fill up on enough junk food, when the real stuff comes along, you will have no room for it. Because she went to the prophet first, the widow found the will to follow His words.

When you need a prophetic word from God—a *rhema* just for you—it is good not to fill up on everyone else's opinions. Human solutions may sound logical, practical, or encouraging, but when God has a word for you—when the Holy Spirit is talking to your soul—it is helpful if you are not so full with what everyone else is saying that you don't have any room to hear Him at all.

The second principle from the choices of the widow is that God responds to your emptiness. God responded to the widow when she had nothing to offer. All she had was one solitary jar of oil. All of her other jars, pots, pans, and containers sat empty. What could she do with one jar of oil? Nothing. She didn't even have anything to mix it with to make some food. She certainly wasn't going to eat it straight.

One of the reasons it is often difficult to experience God's miracles of provision is that we approach Him with our fullness rather than with our emptiness.

One of the reasons it is often difficult to experience God's miracles of provision is that we approach Him with our fullness rather than with our emptiness. We present what we think we have to offer to God rather than recognizing that apart from Him, we are literally nothing (John 15). The Bible has a word for that. It is called pride. The Bible also has a word for emptiness. It is called humility.

Pride is recognizing your own self-sufficiency, while humility is recognizing your own insufficiency. Scripture tells us clearly, "God opposes the proud but gives grace to the humble" (James 4:6). There is no such thing as a proud kingdom woman, because the terms are mutually exclusive. In fact, they cannot coexist because the very definition of pride contradicts the definition of a kingdom woman aligned under the authority and rule of God.

One of the Temptations' songs, "Ain't Too Proud to Beg," should be our theme song as believers in Christ. Because when you get too proud to beg God for what you need or too sufficient to need Him—because you think that you can do it on your own, you can fix it, you can solve it, you can face it—you lose out on His greater power and glory. As a kingdom woman, never be too proud to beg for whatever it is you need from Christ. Admit to Him that you know your own emptiness.

The third important principle from the path of the widow is to give to others what you need God to give to you. Or as we read in the book of Luke, "Give, and it will be given to you. A good measure, pressed down, shaken together and running over, will be poured into your lap. For with the measure you use, it will be measured to you" (6:38).

The word *it* in that verse refers to the thing that you gave. Whatever you want God to do for you, give *it* to someone else. All the widow had was one jar of oil, yet the prophet instructed her to pour her one jar of oil into other people's empty jars. She didn't know what he was going to do with the oil once she poured it out. For all she knew, he was going to ask her to take the jars back to her neighbors and give her oil away. But she did it anyway.

This is the principle that Scripture is referring to when Jesus said, "It is more blessed to give than to receive" (Acts 20:35). What He was saying is that by giving, you open up a channel for which to also receive. In other words, by hoarding—or keeping what you think is yours only—you cut off God's flow to you. If God cannot flow through you to others, then He won't continue flowing to you. A blessing can be defined as experiencing, enjoying, and extending the goodness of God in your life. It includes being used by God to bless others as well.

When the widow committed herself to following the instructions of the prophet by pouring her last bit of oil into her neighbors' empty jars, her emptiness then became full. As she poured, her jar kept refilling so that she was able to keep pouring until "she said to her son, 'Bring me another one.' But he replied, 'There is not a jar left.' Then the oil stopped flowing" (2 Kings 4:6).

You are only going to take this step of faith to give to others what you yourself need if you truly believe that God is your source. Because if God is your source, then the question is not whether you have enough to keep giving to others, but whether you have the faith to believe that He will replenish what you give away in His name.

God has promised to "supply all your needs according to His riches in glory" (Philippians 4:19, NASB) when you love Him and walk according to His will (Romans 8:28). That is a promise you can take to the bank, just as the widow eventually did by selling the accumulated oil and retiring off the profit (2 Kings 4:7).

God Does Not Need a Lot to Do a Lot

The last principle from 2 Kings 4 is simple yet profound. God does not need a lot to do a lot. The little bit of oil that the woman had was more than enough for God to multiply. This principle shows up repeatedly in Scripture. All Moses had was a shepherd's staff with a hook on the end, but when he threw it down and then picked it back up, it became the powerful rod of God. In fact, it was so powerful, Moses used it to open up the Red Sea and bring water out of a rock.

All David had was a slingshot and five smooth stones. In fact, all he used was one of those stones. Yet he defeated the giant that an entire army could not bring down (1 Samuel 17). All Samson had was the jaw of a donkey, and he slew the Philistines (Judges 15). All Shamgar had was an oxgoad, and he saved the entire nation of Israel (Judges 3).

All Rachel had were some jars full of water, but in offering the water to the camels of a stranger, she became a part of the lineage of Jesus Christ, our Savior (Genesis 29). All Sarah had was one son, and she became the mother to the entire nation of God's chosen people (Genesis 21). All Jael had was a tent peg, and she was able to take down Sisera and change the course of an entire battle (Judges 4).

All the young boy who was listening to Jesus' sermon had was some fish and bread. But it was enough to feed everyone and provide leftovers for the disciples to lug around. All Mary Magdalene had was a jar of perfume, yet she taught us one of the greatest spiritual lessons in the Bible.

If you don't have a lot, that's okay. God can take your little and turn it into much when you commit to following His path for you.

If you don't have a lot, that's okay. God can take your little and turn it into much when you commit to following His path for you. In fact, He can do "immeasurably more than all we ask or imagine, according to his power that is at work within us." (Ephesians 3:20).

Being a kingdom woman of commitment involves making a decision based in faith to follow God's prescribed path while aligning yourself under His authority. It will rarely be the path you would have chosen on your own, but it will always lead you to your destiny, which is a far greater place to be than no place at all.

In a memorable poem written in the style of Dr. Seuss, a character named Zoad is similar to so many of us and our inability to commit to a solitary direction by faith:

> *Did I ever tell you about the young Zoad?*
> *Who came to a sign at the fork of the road?*
> *He looked one way and the other way too*
> *The Zoad had to make up his mind what to do—*
> *Well, the Zoad scratched his head, and his chin, and his pants.*
> *And he said to himself, "I'll be taking a chance.*
> *If I go to Place One, that place may be hot*
> *so how will I know if I like it or not?*
> *On the other hand, though, I'll feel such a fool*
> *If I go to Place Two and find it's too cool.*
> *In that case I may catch a chill and turn blue.*
> *So Place One may be best and not Place Two."*
> *"Play safe," cried the Zoad, "I'll play safe, I'm no dunce.*
> *I'll simply start off to both places at once."*
> *And that's how the Zoad, who would not take a chance,*
> *went no place at all with a split in his pants.*[4]

God has given kingdom women the direction and path that He wants you to follow. And if He has not revealed each and every step at this very moment, my advice is to just continue walking until He reveals the next step. God's path is the pathway of faith. Following Him, even if you cannot see the destination up ahead, is the surest way to become all you were created to be. Issues arise, though, if you attempt to mix the world's wisdom with godly wisdom. That is when you end up going no place at all instead of arriving at the destiny uniquely for you.

PART II

THE FAITH
OF A
KINGDOM WOMAN
~ POWER ~

5

The Power of a Kingdom Woman's Faith

A few years ago an interesting event occurred in South Carolina. I was scheduled to speak at a crusade at Williams-Brice Stadium, which is the football stadium of the University of South Carolina. The weather report had predicted rain. In fact, it had said that there would be a storm.

More than twenty-five thousand people had already gathered in the stadium and were waiting for the crusade to begin, when we saw the storm clouds forming. So we, the leaders and organizers of the crusade, wanted to pray that God would hold back the rain.

We went downstairs into a small room, gathered together, and began to pray. Of course, we prayed things like, "Dear God, please hold back the rain" and "If it's Your will, God, could You hold back that rain?"

Yet in the midst of all of us praying, a petite woman named Linda came forward. Perhaps she had gotten frustrated with the prayers of the so-called professionals—the preachers and the leaders.

Whatever the case, Linda stood up and asked, "Do you mind if I pray?"

What else could we say but "Go ahead"?

Linda prayed, "Lord, Your name is at stake. We told these people that if they would come out tonight they would hear a word from God. We told them they would hear from You. Now, if they come and You let it rain, and You don't control the weather, then You will look bad. We told them that You wanted to say something to them, and if You don't keep back what You can control—the weather—someone could say that Your name is no good."

And then she threw in a line that caused us all to look at each other out of the corners of our eyes. "Therefore right now I ask in the Name of the Lord Jesus Christ for the rain to stop for the sake of Your Name!"

With that, we opened our eyes. Eyebrows went up. All we could say and think was "Whoa. Did she really just pray that?"

Following the prayers, we all went up and sat on the platform. The sky had now become entirely black behind us. A guy who had been assigned to communicate directly with the weather bureau said, "The showers are coming. They are heavy thunderstorms, and they are coming right at us."

It is now 7:00 PM, and the music is beginning. It is time to start the crusade when massive thunder and lightning surrounded us. People began to stir in their seats. Some even started to get up and open their umbrellas.

Linda was on the stage with the rest of us. While umbrellas began to go up in the audience, and several on the stage, Linda sat there confident. A quiet look of expectation covered her face.

Then something happened that I have only seen once in my entire life. The rain rushed toward the stadium like a wall of water. Yet when it hit the stadium, it split. Half of the rain went on one side of the stadium. The other half went on the other side. Then it literally met on the other side of the stadium. All the while, Linda sat there with a confident look on her face. The rest of us, the preachers and leaders, just looked at each other. We looked at the rain going around the stadium, then we looked at each other again. Then we looked at Linda. Linda stared straight ahead.

> *When kingdom women become passionate about what God is passionate about, positive change can occur in lives, families, communities, and even our nation.*

Now, this is not a story that someone told me. I was there. In fact, my family was there with me. Not only that, but twenty-five thousand people were there with me too. And all of us saw a miracle that night right in front of our eyes. I believe that God paid special attention to Linda's prayer because she had great faith.

She knew God's name. She understood that His name represented His character. And her prayer appealed to that which mattered most to Him. She knew how to speak God's language.

I believe Linda's prayer ushered in a miracle because she realized that God is passionate for His own reputation. She put her faith in God. Her petite frame held power, simply because she was intimately connected with and invested in God's name. Because the rain moved around the stadium, the crowd was protected so they could hear the gospel and respond with open hearts, having just witnessed a weather phenomenon.

When kingdom women become passionate about what God is passionate about, positive change can occur in lives, families, communities, and even our nation.

Hannah

The Bible contains stories of women who faced seemingly impossible situations. Yet time and time again, these women exhibited a faith arguably stronger than most men in Scripture. Women have a unique capacity for faith, and it is one of the primary ways to advance God's kingdom. The first woman I want to look at is in 1 Samuel. Hannah was barren. She couldn't have any children. In fact, the reason she couldn't have any children is because God Himself had closed her womb (1:5). There wasn't simply a biological limitation in Hannah's life. There was a spiritual reason and God's doing behind her physical reality.

Not only could Hannah not conceive, but she was also living in an unpleasant environment. She lived in a culture where a woman's identity was often closely linked, if not entirely linked, to her ability to bear children. People around Hannah made fun of her. They put her down. One woman in particular disturbed Hannah the most. This was Peninnah. She was also a wife of Hannah's husband, Elkanah.

Her [Hannah's] rival wife taunted her cruelly, rubbing it in and never letting her forget that God had not given her children. This went on year after year. Every time she went to the sanctuary of God she could expect to be taunted. Hannah was reduced to tears and had no appetite. (1:6–7, MSG)

As a result, Hannah turned to God.

Crushed in soul, Hannah prayed to God and cried and cried—inconsolably. Then she made a vow:
>   Oh, God-of-the-Angel-Armies,
>   If you'll take a good, hard look at my pain,
>   If you'll quit neglecting me and go into action for me
>   By giving me a son,
>   I'll give him completely, unreservedly to you.
>   I'll set him apart for a life of holy discipline. (1:10–11, MSG)

In a situation she could not fix, Hannah asked God to reverse the way things had been all of her adult life. Hannah approached her physical problem spiritually. Just like Linda who understood that the storm had less to do with the clouds in the air than it had to do with God's ability to hold back those clouds, Hannah sought her relief and assistance from the only One who could bring it. She sought out a spiritual solution to a physical need.

When Hannah sought God as the solution to her problem, she placed her faith in Him. In fact, she went a step beyond that. She told God that if He would *give* her a son, then she would *give* that same son back to serve Him in the temple all the days of his life. She looked to God as the answer and sought to honor Him in the process. With that, He provided Hannah with a son. The Scripture says,

Early the next morning they arose and worshiped before the LORD and then went back to their home at Ramah. Elkanah lay with Hannah his wife, and *the LORD remembered her.* So in the course of time Hannah conceived and gave birth to a son. She named him Samuel, saying, "Because I asked the LORD for him." (1:19–20)

An important principle of living by faith is knowing that if God is the cause of whatever issue you are facing, then only God can be the solution. It doesn't matter whom you know, what your name is, how powerful you are, or how much money you have. God is your source. Everyone and everything else is just a resource. Because the Lord *remembered* Hannah, her womb was opened.

Hannah kept her word after giving birth to Samuel. She gave him to the Lord for service in the temple. The son whom she had prayed for all of those years was given back to God, just as she said she would do. But what is interesting is that after Hannah gave to God the very thing that she wanted all along—her child—He in turn gave her a home full of children. In 1 Samuel 2, we discover that not only did Hannah give birth to Samuel, but she also went on to give birth to three more sons and two daughters (verse 2:21). Not only did God respond to Hannah's faith by answering her prayer, but

An important principle of living by faith is knowing that if God is the cause of whatever issue you are facing, then only God can be the solution.

He also went beyond her request to fill her home with five children. He honored her act of faith in giving Samuel back to Him.

The Widow of Zarephath

In 1 Kings, we come across another woman who demonstrated the power of faith in the face of impossible odds. A famine had hit the land where she lived, making it difficult for her to survive. The economy had crumbled, and the country was experiencing far more than a recession. It was a depression affecting countless individuals.

God had instructed the prophet Elijah to go to a place called Zarephath, where a widow lived. God told Elijah that He had commanded the widow to provide for Elijah. However, when Elijah met the woman at the gate to the city, he faced reluctance on her part. At first when he asked her for a cup of water, she was willing to give that to him and started to go get it. Yet when he asked for some bread with his water, she wasn't so eager to do that:

> "As surely as the LORD your God lives," she replied, "I don't have any bread—only a handful of flour in a jar and a little oil in a jug. I am gathering a few sticks to take home and make a meal for myself and my son, that we may eat it—and die." (17:12)

The woman did not plan on eating again after this meal. She explained to Elijah that she couldn't give him anything because she didn't have anything to give.

Yet Elijah had gotten a different message from God. God had told Elijah that He had commanded the woman to help Elijah. In that confidence, Elijah instructed the woman to not be afraid. He asked her to go make a bread cake for him, but then he told her something else. See, the woman said she did not have enough. Elijah knew that she was down to her last serving of grain. But Elijah told her that if she would make him a cake, then she could make some for herself and her son as well. There would be enough for all of them.

> For this is what the LORD, the God of Israel, says: "The jar of flour will not be used up and the jug of oil will not run dry until the day the LORD gives rain on the land." (Verse 14)

The widow had no future. She had no savings. She had no provision. She had no hope. Yet in the face of uncertainty and famine, Elijah asked her to demonstrate faith. What did the woman do? Exactly what Elijah told her that God said to do. She obeyed.

I wonder what she must have been thinking as she scooped up the last bit of flour and turned it into a bread cake. Most likely, it wasn't going to be a tasty bread cake. I can't imagine that she had any seasoning at that point, and she definitely didn't have anything to go with it. I'm not sure the word *cake* gives the right impression. It might have looked more like a bread ball when all was said and done. Whatever the case, the widow used what she had left to obey God.

She gave something to a complete stranger over feeding her son. Her maternal instincts must have been screaming at her, yet her faith overrode them. If she was really going to be able to provide a future for her son, she was going to have to ignore the desire to feed him the last bit of food she had left. She was going to have to put all of her eggs, or at least all of her flour, in one basket—God's basket.

Yet when she did, "the jar of flour was not used up and the jug of oil did not run dry, in keeping with the word of the LORD spoken by Elijah" (verse 16).

Elijah's request wasn't practical. In fact, it might not have even seemed moral: to give food intended to feed her son to someone else. What was Elijah thinking to make such a high demand? He knew that the God who instructed him to do so would make good on His word.

It didn't make sense. In fact, it was downright ridiculous. Yet God had asked. And she obeyed in faith. She had the faith of Linda. The faith of Hannah. She had faith that would bring heaven down to earth.

This is my take on the passage: God knew about this particular woman's faith and that is why He sent Elijah to her. There were many widows at that time. The famine had gone on for almost four years. But not every widow gained God's attention, because not every widow demonstrated a heart of faith. Somewhere along the line, God had seen this widow act in faith. He knew that if He asked her to do what seemed entirely unreasonable, but which would bring His blessing and favor, she would do it.

He didn't choose her randomly. Her actions, thoughts, and decisions leading up to that point had made her a woman who caught God's special attention. Besides that, she lived outside of Israel in the Phoenician city of Sidon. God didn't go to the "church" to find the woman He was going to use. He didn't go down and visit the nearest Bible study. This is because sometimes the greatest faith is found in the most surprising places, simply because faith depends upon relationship rather than religion. Religion can be one of the greatest hindrances to faith because it creates dependency on a ritual rather than on the God of the universe who can do all things.

When looking for a woman of great and powerful faith, God looked beyond the pew. He looked into hearts to find the one woman who would respond. In fact, when God looked for someone to ultimately save the ministry of His prophet Elijah at a time of great trial and need, He didn't even go to a man. There certainly were many men at that time with access to some food. Yet at this crucial moment in Elijah's calling as a prophet, God intentionally singled out a kingdom woman to save the day.

Sometimes the greatest faith is found in the most surprising places.

Jesus spoke about the widow in Zarephath, specifically highlighting the fact that God sent Elijah to a woman for help in a crunch time in his ministry:

> I assure you that there were many widows in Israel in Elijah's time, when the sky was shut for three and a half years and there was a severe famine throughout the land. Yet Elijah was not sent to any of them, but to a widow in Zarephath in the region of Sidon. (Luke 4:25–26)

In other words, God knew that when times had gotten tough and each person was trying to survive, the church folk's faith wasn't going to be strong enough to do what He was going to ask. The women of Israel, the ladies who had been raised to trust in the Lord with all their hearts, weren't going to believe His words. Nor would the men. But the foreigner, a woman living outside of the normal "Christian" circles, was the one who would believe. So she got the supernatural intervention in a very hopeless and desperate scenario. She got the supernatural investment from God that would last until the natural investment—the rain—would once again bring food.

I don't think this woman would be the first woman many people conjure up when they consider women of great faith. As a widow living in a time of famine, she was no doubt discouraged and forlorn. Her clothes were probably tattered. Her shoes, if she had any, probably had holes. I don't know what she used to make the bread, perhaps a bowl that was chipped or broken, over coals that barely had anything left to give. Whatever container she used, it wouldn't have made it into any department store for sale or fine restaurant to use for cooking. But when coupled with faith, what seemed like not enough became the very avenue for more than enough.

Often faith involves looking beyond what you can see or the limitations that you face. Maybe you don't have enough time in the day to do all you need to do. Or maybe you really don't have any resources to carry out all that needs to be done. It could be that you are struggling to raise your kids all alone while your husband is busy working or traveling or the children's father has long been out of the picture altogether. Maybe your bank account is low, and you are doing all you can to find a job, and God is asking you to still honor Him with a portion of your money. Or it could be that you have received a report from your doctor that is not good, but God has placed the hope in your heart to believe in His healing touch.

> *Faith acts on the truth that even though you don't have enough, God has more than enough, and He has promised to supply all that you need.*

Maybe God has made it clear to you that He wants you to walk away from your career and stay home full-time with your children, but your family cannot make it on only one income. Or maybe God told you to give away that bonus you got this year to a nearby family in need. Whatever the case, faith acts on the truth that even though you don't have enough, God has more than enough, and He has promised to supply all that you need.

Chrystal's Chronicles

As I write this reflection, I am so very blessed to still have both of my grandmothers alive and available to speak into my life on a regular basis. My maternal grandmother, "Grandma," will be ninety-four soon, and she is planning to embark on yet another cruise in a few weeks. My paternal grandmother, "Two Mama," calls me without fail if she feels like I've gone too long without calling her. If she doesn't call, she sends me an e-mail in ALL CAPS, clearly conveying her disapproval of my lack of communication. Yes. At almost eighty years of age, my grandmother sends e-mails to me.

Both of my grandmothers are alive and kicking.

But since time waits for no one, I'm conscious that the time I have with each of them is precious and that every phone call, every visit, and every kiss on a well-worn cheek is a priceless gift.

The funny thing about watching grandparents or parents age is that I see the people in my life who have always been the strongest, the most in-charge, and the most together slowly morphing before my eyes. They move from a state of perceived independence into a season of dependence.

Recently, my lovely Two Mama has had some health challenges. After years of being a diabetic and having multiple surgeries to maintain good blood flow to her extremities, Two Mama had to have one of her legs amputated. She had gone to the hospital in so much pain. And she's a strong woman, so if she said she was hurting, it must have been really bad. Over the next couple of days, her doctor determined that nothing else could be done to save the leg.

I wasn't there. I couldn't hold her hand. So I did the next best thing and called many times a day. On one of those phone calls, I could hear her crying out in anguish. The pain was just too much, and I heard my strong grandmother expressing that guttural sound that only true agony knows. My dad, who was in the room with her at the time, put the phone to her ear and told me to talk.

"Two Mama, I love you. I'm sorry you are in so much pain. We all love you and are praying that all will be well soon. It's gonna be okay. You are gonna be okay."

In between her waves of throbbing trauma, I heard her say, "God is good, baby. I have to trust Him. God is good."

Where does someone get that kind of faith? Where does a woman find the strength to speak well of her God in the middle of intense pain, hurt, distress, discomfort, or difficulty?

I still consider myself to be in the middle of my own faith walk and don't have the strong fortress of faith my grandmothers have both attained in the face of a lifetime's exposure to good and not-so-good times. However, I know this to be true: The kind of faith my grandmother showed that day and in the days ahead is the kind of faith that can only be built brick by brick and day by day as a woman walks committed to God's purposes and plans for her life.

Hebrews 11:1 defines *faith* as "being sure of what we hope for and certain of what we do not see." *The Message* defines it this way: "The firm foundation under everything that makes life worth living. It's our handle on what we can't see."

Why did my grandmother have the ability to speak well of God in a difficult circumstance? Because she chose to. It's that simple. Not necessarily easy. But definitely simple.

Faith is a decision.

Faith is a decision you make to believe the best about your spouse when you feel deep disappointment about who he appears to be.

Faith is a decision you make to believe that you are who God says you are even when you struggle regularly with insecurity and self-doubt.

Faith is a decision you make to believe that handling your money God's way is the best way.

> *Faith is a decision you make to believe that the dark road you are traveling on will eventually yield to a sunrise.*

Faith is a decision you make to believe that making time to pray about your concerns is a better use of your time than worrying about them.

Faith is a decision you make to believe that the dark road you are traveling on will eventually yield to a sunrise.

Faith is the decision to meditate on, repeat, and rehearse what God says about you and your life—despite what you see.

Just as my grandmother chose to believe in the goodness of God when there was absolutely nothing good about her situation, every true woman of faith must do the same.

A kingdom woman does hard things, and sometimes having faith based on God's Word is the simplest yet toughest thing she will ever have to do.

My mom's mother, Grandma, has seen the object of her faith come to be. She is a mother of eight children, all of whom know Jesus as their personal Savior. That didn't happen by accident. My grandmother spent much of her time raising children alone because my grandfather's job kept him away much of the time. She had the task of caring for the children not only physically but also for their souls.

My mother and her siblings still remember fondly the morning Bible studies that my grandmother led, where she expected them to respectfully listen to God's Word and her discussion of the text. She did this with children who struggled to sit still, children who would sometimes giggle or contract a case of the "sillies," and even teenagers who thought they might have better things to do. My grandmother read the Bible consistently to them for years because she had faith—faith that God's Word would not return void and that she would live to see her children love and serve the Lord. It wasn't easy, but she did it.

These stories of my grandmother with children on her knee encourage me in the season that I'm in. Motherhood is a job that can have a twenty-plus-year wait for the first paycheck. But it is a little easier to press through the wiggles and giggles or the blank stares of the young adults under my roof because I know that I'm not the first one to walk this road.

And you are not the first woman to walk the road you travel either.

The faith we must have as Christian women develops best in the incubator of a community of women whose faith walks have taken them a little farther down the road than we currently are. I hope you have women in your life who can encourage you to keep walking forward when the streetlights are off and your flashlight is broken.

Even if you don't feel like you have that kind of sisterhood, God's Word is full of stories of women who walked the same path. Those women found out that it is worthwhile to trust that God is who He says He is and that He will do what He says He can do.

Like Rahab, believe God to set you free from a lifestyle that does not please Him.

Like Hannah, believe that God hears the guttural longings of your soul.

Like Ruth, believe that God can carry you through devastation and loss so you can dance again.

Like Bathsheba, believe that God's goodness can supersede the consequences of a bad decision.

Like the woman at the well, believe that God can satisfy your deepest thirst.

Like Mary, the woman with the expensive perfume, believe that to offer Jesus the best of everything you are and everything you have is never a worthless pursuit.

Like Mary, the mother of Jesus, believe that God can use regular gals like you and me to deliver great things to the rest of the world or to the mission field within our own homes.

Yes, I am blessed to have both of my grandmothers with me and to see the fruit of their faith as well as their continual practice of faith in God—who He is and what they know He can do.

You are blessed because that same God is *your* God: "Know therefore that the LORD your God is God; he is the faithful God, keeping his covenant of love to a thousand generations of those who love him and keep his commands" (Deuteronomy 7:9).

Even when it hurts, God is with you. Even when it's hard, God can help you. Even when things seem out of control, God is for you.

He hears every cry and sees every tear. He is not absent when you are in a state of anguish or anxiety. He knows that you don't want to travel your road alone. He is not off duty, on leave, or MIA. He knows that He has asked you for high sacrifice, hard choices, or to carry a heavy cross.

Have faith. And if all you can conjure up is a mustard seed's worth, that's enough.

Act Out

Even though your faith may be small, let your actions be big. Step out and praise God in spite of the trial you may be facing. Step out and stand on God's Word, even when it might not make sense to the people around you. More than that, step out in faith and offer help to others who might be struggling similarly to you. Choose to honor God by giving Him something that is near and dear to you. Whether you sacrifice your own time, energy, or a personal want, nothing is wasted when you commit it to serving Him.

Whether you sacrifice your own time, energy, or a personal want, nothing is wasted when you commit it to serving Him.

Kingdom women understand that one of the secrets to a life full of the power of faith is to honor God by what you give to Him and what you give to others in His name. Luke 6:38 is frequently quoted, but few people truly understand it. We looked at it briefly in the last chapter, but let's take a closer look now:

> Give, and it will be given to you. Good measure, pressed down, shaken together, running over, will be put into your lap. For with the measure you use it will be measured back to you. (ESV)

This one verse summarizes the core of both women we covered earlier in this chapter. To get something in return for their faith, both Hannah and the widow had to give something. Hannah made the commitment to God that she would give up her son if God would give her one. The widow had to give away all she had left to eat.

Other kingdom women in the Bible did similar things. In fact, we looked at Ruth earlier in the book. She gave up the potential for a relationship with men in her own culture. It would have been much easier for Ruth to find another man in her own country than as a foreigner in another country. Yet she told Naomi, her mother-in-law, that she was going to give up that option and go with Naomi instead. Ruth told Naomi that her people would be Ruth's people, too. She said that Naomi's God would be Ruth's God. Ruth made a kingdom-based decision to follow the one true God above any personal or convenience-based plans she might have had.

Ruth had a need: She was alone; perhaps she was even lonely. But rather than sit home and try to position herself in the best way she could to meet that need, she gave the very thing that she needed to someone else. As an elderly widow, Naomi had very little chance, if any at all, of ever marrying again. Naomi was in fact more alone than Ruth. Because of this reality, Ruth chose to meet Naomi's relational need. And in giving "it" to Naomi, Ruth received "it" from God in the form of a new husband, Boaz.

In 1 Samuel we saw that Hannah had gone for years without a child because God had closed her womb. Yet Hannah's situation changed when she wept bitterly before the Lord and vowed to Him that she would give "it"—her child—to Him if He would give "it," a child, to her. She gave up her son before God even gave her one.

When Hannah gave "it" (her need) to the service of God, God gave "it" back to her because He opened her womb so much that she went on to have five more children.

The widow of Zarephath needed food. God said to give "it" to the prophet. Even though it wasn't practical to give the very thing she needed to the prophet, the widow did just that in faith. She gave her food, and in return, God gave "it" back. He gave her more than enough to eat until the famine ended, and she was able to once again grow her own food.

Faith isn't simply tied to belief. It is tied to an action. Faith is tied to your feet. The power of faith comes when you are willing to give the very thing that you need to someone else so God can give "it" back to you. The reason why so many prayers go unanswered is simply because people are not willing to give God all they have. They are not willing to give the very thing that they are searching for and in need of. Give, and *it* will be given to you in this lifetime. Pressed down, shaken together, and running over.

To better understand what is meant by the last phrase we need to know that in biblical days, a woman would wear a robe that had a special fold sewn into it. This fold served much like an apron today. When a woman would go get grain, she would hold out the portion of her robe with the fold, and the grain would be poured into her lap, so to speak.

The reason why so many prayers go unanswered is simply because people are not willing to give God all they have.

Because she wanted her robe to hold as much grain as possible, she would shake her apron to settle the grain into all the open spaces. Shaking created more room for more grain. Then she would press down the grain to flatten it some more so the robe could hold even more grain until it finally was running over.[1]

What God is saying is that when you give according to the faith you have in Him, He will raise up someone to give "it" back to you so much so that it will run over. You will receive back in abundance.

The power of faith is not just that God will answer your prayer; the power of faith in action is that God will give back to you "far more abundantly than all that we ask or think" (Ephesians 3:20, esv).

Faith is not a principle to be analyzed. Living as a kingdom woman of faith is a principle to be experienced. Linda had heard the weather report like all of us. She could see the clouds. Yet Linda knew the power of God. She knew that the crusade was meant to bless the thousands in attendance and glorify God's name. It wasn't her crusade. It was for others to know the blessing of God. Because of that, Linda prayed in faith.

I'll never forget when the gentleman sitting next to Linda on the stadium stage offered her his umbrella as the dark storm clouds rolled in. She turned and looked at him, smiled politely, and then put up her hand. "I don't need it," she said.

And she didn't. Actually, none of us did.

6

THE PURSUIT OF A KINGDOM WOMAN'S FAITH

One time I was battling a cold and couldn't shake it. I called my doctor and told him my symptoms, and he told me I didn't need to come in. He was going to call in a prescription for me. He told me what medicine he was prescribing and how to take it.

Now, a number of things went into motion. First, I had to believe that I was talking to the person I thought I had called, because I couldn't see him. It was just a conversation over the phone. So I had to listen to his voice. I listened, and he told me how to fix my problem. I could have stayed in bed and meditated. I could have believed him but stayed in bed thinking about how good it was that I had a doctor who understood my problem and provided me with a solution. I could have lain there thinking how great it was that I had a solution. But all that lying around and thinking about the doctor's words wouldn't have made me better. It might have given me warm fuzzies because he personally talked to me, but I'd still have been just as sick as I was when I first called him. I had to get up, get in my car, drive to Walgreens, and ask the pharmacist, "Do you have a prescription with my name on it?"

While there are many kinds of medicine in the pharmacy, I needed something with my name on it. The doctor had told me it was there, and I acted on his word.

Beyond that, I could have just received the medicine and looked at it. I could have made sure that it looked acceptable to me. But I'd still have been just as sick. By following the doctor's instructions, my belief was matching up with my works, and I began to feel much better.

A lot of us have spiritual colds, yet we come to God to hear what the Doctor has to prescribe, only to have nothing change. This is because many of us stop there. We think about how good it was to hear from Him or to talk to Him. Some of us turn to the Word of God and feel good about how wonderful the prescription sounds and all of the things that it is supposed to do, but we stay just as "sick" because we don't ingest the "medicine" God gives us.

The pursuit of faith involves much more than simply seeking God and His Word. While those are definitely a part of it, true pursuit involves responding in such a way that our actions follow His instructions. Only when faith comes full circle will the full benefit be manifested in our lives. Full faith is an all-out, no-holds-barred approach to a life punctuated by actions of belief.

Full faith is an all-out, no-holds-barred approach to a life punctuated by actions of belief.

I realize that things happen that make it more of a challenge to live with actions that demonstrate faith. Perhaps you weren't raised in an environment where the people around you taught you what a life of faith looked like. Perhaps your life revealed disappointments early on, or maybe you were hurt in some way and are a little "gun-shy" about taking chances. Maybe you think you have too much to lose by stepping out in a direction that you sense God is leading you. Whatever it is, people have different reasons why they shrink back from trusting and relying on God.

Scripture tells of a woman who also had challenges, but she was able to overcome those *because* of her faith. She didn't allow anything to stand in the way of doing what she needed to do. In the King James Version, this woman's primary problem was "an issue of blood":

A woman having an *issue of blood* twelve years, which had spent all her living upon physicians, neither could be healed of any, came behind [Jesus], and touched the border of his garment: and immediately her issue of blood stanched. And Jesus said, Who touched me? When all denied, Peter and they that were with him said, Master, the multitude throng thee and press thee, and sayest thou, Who touched me? (Luke 8:43–45, KJV)

Bleeding, in particular, is a difficult issue to deal with because the loss of blood means the loss of life—zest, energy, and strength—because "the life of the flesh is in the blood" (Liviticus 17:11, KJV). I'm sure you've heard the phrase *bleeding out*, meaning that a person has lost so much blood that he or she dies. The body needs blood in order to live.

Blood is an important part of life. Whenever you go to the doctor because you are not well, often he or she will take a blood test. A doctor can discover a lot by looking at and examining your blood. Because within your blood is the essence of life itself.

This woman was hemorrhaging; her life had been ebbing away from her for twelve very long years. Yet not only was her physical life ebbing away because of this issue—undoubtedly making her weak and putting her organs in pain as they lacked the necessary oxygen to function properly—but her finances were being hit as well.

Some of you reading these words right now know what it is like to have ongoing doctor's bills because a health issue continues to go unfixed for a prolonged period of time. As the doctors try this, that, and the other, the bills continue to tax and strain your finances.

Yet not only did this woman suffer from a physical and a financial problem; she also suffered from a spiritual problem. We know this because she was a Jewish woman living under the Old Testament law:

If a woman [has] an issue of her blood many days out of the time of her separation, or if it [runs] beyond the time of her separation; all the days of the issue of her uncleanness shall be as the days of her separation: she shall be unclean. (Leviticus 15:25, KJV)

To be considered "unclean" in Israelite culture carried with it multiple ramifications. For one, she could not be touched. This meant that her physical problem also bled into a social problem because she was forced to live apart from the touch or warmth of humanity. Most likely, she couldn't go out and take part in marketplace activities, since any other woman who might accidentally touch her could be considered unclean as well. She also couldn't attend any religious ceremonies. She had probably also been prescribed a number of tonics to cure her hemorrhage, and those may have come with some side effects of their own. Most likely this woman lived a lonely, isolated, and painful existence. She definitely had "issues."

Before we dive deeper into her story, though, I want to pause to ask if you can relate to this woman. Perhaps not on the entire scale of her story, but has something impacted you physically, socially, financially, or spiritually, and whatever you try to fix the problem, it just doesn't work? You spend your money on medical help, psychological help, vitamins, herbs, and the latest cure-alls. Regardless of all of that, you are left with an empty purse and a heavy heart as you quietly carry your burden.

The faithful woman needed a supernatural healing. So she made her way to a position where she could get just that.

If that describes you in any way—aching, hurting, discouraged, despondent, disappointed—and it doesn't seem like anyone can help—in fact, what help you do get tends to make things even worse—I want to ask you to learn from this woman.

After twelve years, there is no doubt that her situation appeared unfixable from a human point of view. In fact, it's even doubtful that she felt like anyone even cared anymore. If things were going to get better, something beyond her and beyond everyone and everything else had to happen. She needed a supernatural touch. The faithful woman needed a supernatural healing. So she made her way to a position where she could get just that.

As we saw earlier in Luke 8, she made her way through the crowds and came up behind Jesus to touch His cloak. Matthew 9:20 said she specifically reached for the hem of Christ's garment. Why is that important? Because to go low enough to touch the hem, she needed to humble herself. She needed to relinquish all forms of pride, self-preservation, and human wisdom. She had to humble herself to open herself to being impacted by God's Word—God's viewpoint on her issue. She had to lean not on her own understanding (Proverbs 3:5) but lean down to gain God's understanding. She had to stop looking at her situation through her own perspective and start looking for God's solution. She believed that if she could just get hold of that hem, attached to Jesus Christ—the Son of God and the Word of God—she would be healed.

We know she was a woman of great faith: "She said to herself, 'If I only touch his cloak, I will be healed' " (Matthew 9:21).

A kingdom woman is a woman who knows and believes that her solution is not found in money, human reasoning, or other people. Her solution is found in humbling herself before Jesus Christ and surrendering to the Word of God. Many times, God will let you try everything you think you need to try to fix your own issues. He will let you spend all of your money, waste all of your time, and simply become worn out and weary. He allows this because often it isn't until someone has come to the end of herself and her own options that she looks to the only true option for lasting healing—God.

The important thing to note in this kingdom woman's story is that she understood the power of connecting Jesus Christ with the Word of God. See, if you have the written Word yet no living Word, you have truth without life. If you have the living Word at the exclusion of the written Word, you have life without the full revelation of truth. But when you have the living Word while grabbing hold of the written Word, you have life and truth. In pursuing that combination in faith, the woman was healed immediately.

Chrystal's Chronicles

Pine Cove, in Tyler, Texas, is a Christian camp that our family has attended every year for as long as I can remember. My dad is often a featured speaker at Pine Cove, so when he is, the rest of us tag along for a nice family vacation. A few years ago, however, our vacation took a scary turn.

One afternoon, the kids had finished their activities, and it was time for them to settle in for a nap. Our week together was coming to a close, and the women in our family decided to take a trip into town to shop while our little ones slept. We left them in the cabin with their granddad, whom they affectionately call "Poppy." I remember that we left around 2:30 PM. As I backed out of the driveway, I remember seeing my oldest son, Jesse, watching me through the window in the room where he was supposed to be lying down.

Around 4:00 PM I got a call from my dad saying that the front door to the cabin was open and that three-year-old Jesse wasn't in the house. My dad had checked everywhere and couldn't find my son anywhere. At that moment, my heartbeat went into overdrive, and my lungs tightened. I could hardly take in air. If you have ever thought for a second that your child was lost, had disappeared, or might be in danger, then you know exactly what I'm talking about. I prayed the only words I could muster at the moment: "Lord Jesus . . . please help."

I told myself that I needed to keep calm, trust in God, and do whatever I needed to find my son. We gathered the girls from our various locations in the shopping center and immediately rushed back to the camp to help out with the frantic search for my baby boy.

We were twenty minutes away from the camp. Those twenty minutes crept insanely slow. I wanted the phone to ring, and I wanted my dad to be on the other end of the line telling me that he found Jesse in another room or outside playing in the dirt. Instead, I got a call from him to tell me that camp personnel had been assembled to begin a search in the woods and around the lake that sits in the center of the campground.

In those moments, I must admit, my faith was not working. I tried. I wanted to believe. But a million images flashed through my mind, and the stories of other families that I'd watched play out on television came to my thoughts. Those long minutes were probably the most intense I have ever faced. My heart was tearing apart on the inside.

While we were still en route, and even before the search began, a phone call came from the police station. A police officer had found Jesse. He was safe, happy, and ready to come home.

From what we can piece together, Jesse must have run out of the room and out of the front door in an attempt to catch us as we left for our shopping trip. My dad had been in his room with his door open so he could listen for the kids, but with the commotion of all of us women leaving the cabin, he hadn't heard anything unusual when my son went out the door as well. Some time after Jesse left the cabin, the police picked him up from some people who had found him wandering alone.

Jesse had walked out of the cabin, off the campground, and onto the main road—a two-lane rural road on which vehicles typically travel between fifty and sixty miles per hour. He left the cabin wearing only a diaper—no socks and no shirt. A car passed by him, and he ran out into the road behind the car. It could have been that the car resembled our car. I'm not sure. Whatever the case, Jesse began pursuing the car on the road. The driver in the car saw in his rearview mirror the small, diaper-clad child running to catch him. He pulled over immediately. This unnamed driver picked him up and took him to the nearest house on the road. From there, the residents called the police, and the quest began to find out whose three-year-old, unclothed kid this was.

Before the police even arrived, a member of the Pine Cove staff heading to town noticed the commotion and stopped to find out what was going on. The staff member knew that the speaker for Pine Cove was my dad and that he had brought his entire family with him. The staff person suggested that my son might belong to the Evans family. When the police arrived, they brought Jesse back to the camp and tracked us down. By the time I arrived on the grounds, Jesse was dressed, playing with a stuffed animal the police officer had given him, and enjoying all the attention. I ran to Jesse and picked him up in my arms. I hoped I didn't hurt him because I was squeezing him so hard. The first words out of my baby's mouth were, "Mommy, I found you!"

The police told us that Jesse had been happy. However, the officers also said they could tell that he had been crying at one point, because dried tears were on his face. But from the time he had chased after the car on the road and the family had picked him up, he had been smiling and laughing.

Later that evening, I asked Jesse why he had left the house.

He said without hesitation, "I was looking for you, Mommy."

My young son had been looking for me. He had been pursuing me. He had seen me head off in another direction in a crowd of aunties and relatives, and he had to do everything he could to find me. This eventually led him to a road where his three-year-old legs chased after a car. Had Jesse realized that he couldn't find me and that he was alone somewhere, he might have just stood by himself and cried.

He might have just sat down and given up. Yet because he kept pursuing—he kept looking for anything that resembled what he was searching for—he chased down a car, the driver stopped, and Jesse eventually "found" me.

I'm convinced that Jesus Christ was right there with little Jesse, encouraging him to keep looking, keep pursuing. Even though he had wandered out into a frightening and dangerous scenario, because he did not quit pursuing what he believed he would find, he found what he was looking for.

"Mommy, I found you!" Those words still bring tears to my eyes and clog up my throat with gratitude for a child who kept looking—and for a God who stayed right there with him the entire way.

I don't know what you are looking for. I don't know the object of your deepest desires. You may know exactly what you want, or you may simply be struggling with a hole that you don't know how to fill. Either way, there is one thing that I know for certain. Pursuing God is worth it. Be determined to know nothing "except Jesus Christ and him crucified" (1 Corinthians 2:2).

God can deliver to us more than we could ever acquire on our own without Him.

When asked about the most important thing that a person should do, Jesus responded, "Love the Lord your God with all your heart and with all your soul and with all your mind and with all your strength" (Mark 12:30). To chase after God, to want more of Him over and above all else, is where the journey of faith begins. When we show by our actions that we believe that He is good, and we illustrate by our activity that believe that God can deliver to us more than we could ever acquire on our own without Him, that is the beginning of the journey of faith.

Who Touched Me?

All little Jesse knew when he saw his mom pull out of the driveway was that he wanted to find her. In his tiny three-year-old mind, he decided to pursue her the only way he knew how—on his tiny three-year-old feet. Although the situation in real-time was probably the most frightening moment of my life, the purity of the illustration of passionately pursuing the one you love—in Jesse's case, his mom, Chrystal—is such a great reminder to each of us about how we are to want nothing more than to be in Christ's presence. How we are to willingly leave the security of our comfort zone and step out in faith to pursue the path that will take us the closest to Jesus.

It was no small step for the woman who suffered from hemorrhaging to move through a crowd that normally would reject her and scorn her as an untouchable outcast. She courageously pursued Christ even though it took her out of the comfort of obscurity. And because she did, she found Him, along with her miracle.

One of the most intriguing elements of the story of this woman is how Jesus was able to tell, apart from all the others, who was touching Him when this particular woman touched His clothes. He could feel His power being used to heal her:

> "Who touched me?" Jesus asked.
>
> When they all denied it, Peter said, "Master, the people are crowding and pressing against you."
>
> But Jesus said, "Someone touched me; I know that power has gone out from me." (Luke 8:45–46)

Keep in mind that there is one fundamental difference between the woman touching Jesus and everyone else who was pressing up against Him and touching Him in some form or fashion. I want to again point out this difference because it is a spiritual principle that, when applied, will open up the gateway of heaven's power in your life as a kingdom woman: *The woman who touched the hem of Christ's garment lowered herself; probably she knelt.*

She had humbled herself to pursue the very object of her faith, the Word of God. Everyone else was standing up. They were part of the crowd, content to approach Jesus at the same level and deeply unaware of their authentic need for His Word. A large number of people in the crowd touched or pressed against Jesus yet did not receive any manifestation of His power.

See, you can be part of a crowd who gathers at church or even comes together to do a Bible study, but unless you recognize your true humility before the living God and your complete dependence on Him and His Word, you will only be in the vicinity. You will only be part of the Jesus Fan Club. You will go untouched. Nothing will change within you because His power will not be released to you.

A kingdom woman of faith must pursue both Christ and the authority of the Scripture with a heart of humility. It is only when you kneel down to reach for the hem, when you humble yourself under His divine authority based on His divine Word, that you will get the power you need to live out the fullness of your destiny.

> *A kingdom woman of faith must pursue both Christ and the authority of the Scripture with a heart of humility.*

You can get a touch from Jesus right now if you are willing to go low enough, if you are willing to ignore the stares of the people, and if you are willing to press on through your pain. If you will humble yourself to grab hold of His Word, His power is yours.

As a pastor of a fairly large congregation, I see a certain pattern play out too often. I see individuals who long to be healed, to be set free, and to serve God, yet they won't relinquish their control, their self-dependence and preservation. They won't let go and go low. As a result, they remain in the vicinity without the power they need to live a victorious life.

Faith coupled with humility is the secret to every kingdom woman's success. As one theologian wrote, "Pride must die in you, or nothing of heaven can live in you."[1] Because the woman who struggled for twelve years with a major health issue chose the path of greatest humility before God, she received the greatest gift of power and healing.

In fact, kneeling down to touch the blue cords tied to the hem of Jesus' garment wasn't the end of her practice of humility. Following the transfer of healing power to the woman, Jesus asked who had touched her. He wasn't asking because He didn't know. He was asking because He wanted the woman to do one more brave act of humble faith. He wanted her to go public. He knew she had been healed. She knew she had been healed. In fact Mark 5:29 says, "She felt in her body that she was freed from her suffering."

He wanted her to share with the others what had happened as a result of her great humility and faith. He wanted her to step out of the comfort zone of the isolated life she had known for so long and publicly declare what He had done. Jesus knew that this action would not come naturally to a woman who was used to being overlooked and ignored. He knew that speaking up about what had happened would be uncomfortable for her. But He wanted her to do it. Even in doing it once, in His presence, she would learn the courage to do it again and again. This woman of great faith and humility also needed to discover great courage. And Jesus was right there to help her. When she heard Him asking specifically for her . . .

> Then the woman, seeing that she could not go unnoticed, came trembling and fell at his feet. In the presence of all the people, she told why she had touched him and how she had been instantly healed. (Luke 8:47)

She trembled. She wasn't used to being noticed in large crowds. She wasn't used to being a part of a conversation in the public's eye. But she came forward and told Jesus she had touched His clothing. Jesus' response was personal. She was not a stranger to Him at all. In fact, He called her the endearing term in that culture of *daughter*. He rewarded both her pursuit and her courage with more than healing. He rewarded it with peace, saying, "Daughter, your faith has healed you. Go in peace" (verse 48).

Somehow between getting physically healed and having the courage to testify about it, she had established a relationship with her Savior. She had gone from "Who?" to "Daughter." She became a recipient of peace within the family of God.

Not everyone gets peace in this life. Many people have what would be considered the blessings of good health, money, clothes, or a nice house. Yet God can bless you with a house, and you still may not have a home. God can bless you with physical healing, but you may still be in mental anguish. God can bless you with things that your physical five senses can enjoy, but you still may not have a relationship with Him.

Jesus wants to do more for you. He doesn't mind giving you stuff. He

Things that you have been struggling with for years may be resolved in a moment when you pursue Christ humbly, publicly, and holistically.

doesn't mind your body working properly. And He wants you to be well. But more than that, He wants you to be His daughter. He wants you to have the courage to pursue Him publicly in order to enter into an intimate relationship with Him.

A kingdom woman pursues Christ in private and in public. That's when you get to see Him show up in a way that you cannot explain. That's when you get to experience a closeness you have never known. Pursuing Jesus while you grab hold of His Word releases power to you. Things that you have been struggling with for years may be resolved in a moment when you pursue Christ humbly, publicly, and holistically.

7

THE POSSIBILITIES
OF A KINGDOM
WOMAN'S FAITH

The story goes it had been a hard winter in the Rockies. The snow piled deeper and deeper. The temperature dropped below zero and stayed there. The rivers froze over. People were suffering.

The Red Cross used helicopters to fly in supplies. After a long, hard day, as they were returning to their base camp, the rescue team in a helicopter saw a cabin nearly submerged in the snow. A thin wisp of smoke came from the chimney. The men figured the people in the cabin were probably critically short of food and fuel.

Because of the trees, they had to set down about a mile from the cabin. They put their heavy emergency equipment on their backs, trudged through waist-deep snow, and reached the cabin exhausted, panting, and perspiring. They pounded on the door, and a thin, gaunt mountain woman finally answered.

The lead man barely could get the words out, "Ma'am, we're from the Red Cross."

She was silent for a moment, and then she said, "It's been a hard, long winter, sonny. I just don't think we can give anything this year."

Many women find themselves in situations like this mountain woman. It seems like you've used every ounce of energy, supply, reserve, and know-how just to meet the needs of those around you, and yet someone still comes knocking at your door. The problem is that it becomes difficult to discern that that person is not there to ask for more but to offer help. While the Red Cross had actually shown up to assist the woman, she assumed that they were just others in a long line of people needing something from her.

Sometimes it is difficult to distinguish when God is sending help your way, because it comes wrapped in a shroud of faith. It takes an unveiling before you realize what God is actually up to. Many women in the Bible had to step out in faith when they faced a lack or need before they saw God's response to meet their needs with abundance. The phrase *taking a leap of faith* implies a swift and sure movement in a direction where the destination is unseen.

> *The phrase* taking a leap of faith *implies a swift and sure movement in a direction where the destination is unseen.*

In 2011 I was in South Africa with Lois, and we saw a beautiful animal called the impala. The impala has the unique ability to jump over ten feet high. It also is able to leap farther than thirty feet. In Africa, the impala runs and leaps freely in wide-open game parks or wildlife preserves. However, the impala—despite its gift of leaping high and long—can easily be contained in a zoo enclosure with nothing more than a three-foot-high wall. This is because the impala does not jump when it cannot visualize where it will land. The impala remains trapped in self-imposed limitations simply because of its inability to take a *leap of faith*.

For many of us, faith is an amorphous term we just can't seem to grasp. Because we lack faith, we stay confined behind walls of fear, doubt, insecurity, and self-preservation. Yet faith is the very footpath to freedom. Simply put, faith is acting like God is telling the truth. To act like God is telling the truth is to act on His words without having to see any proof first that what He says is true. I will often summarize faith in this way: *Faith is acting like something* is *so, even when it is* not *so, in order that it might* be *so simply because God said so.*

Faith is not first and foremost your feelings. It is not an emotion. In fact, many people can *feel* full of faith but have no faith at all. This is because faith is not functional and useful until it is an action. Faith always involves your feet. This is why Paul said to walk by faith—not to talk by faith. You know that you have faith by what you do, not merely by what you say or feel.

Chrystal's Chronicles

My oldest daughter, Kariss, was enrolled in a homeschool co-op during her teenage years. She would receive homework assignments via e-mail from her Fitness and Nutrition teacher. Because Kariss was homeschooled, her responsibility was to complete her assignment before the next week when her class met. My job was to find ways of working in fitness (PE) and nutrition (eating healthy) to our everyday lives. The assignment for one particular week was to do the following:

- Run/walk a mile, and time it.
- Immediately after finishing your mile, count your heart rate.
- Find your target heart rate and target-heart-rate range.

So we went as a family that evening to 24 Hour Fitness and proceeded to do our own workouts. My husband and daughter ran side by side on their respective treadmills to make that one-mile benchmark.

I was on an elliptical machine that put my back to them. Every now and then, I would glance back to see how they were doing. Noticing that my daughter kept reaching for her neck to find her pulse, I worried for a brief second that something was wrong. But then I remembered that she was trying to keep a tab on her pulse while she ran. Funny, you would think that a person running a mile would only be focused on the mile. You would think that the focus would be on putting one foot in front of the other, keeping one's breathing rhythmic, and inhaling deeply. But, oh no, this girl had her hand on her neck.

I find this funny because in the Christian walk, we have so many measurements of how well we are doing in our journey. We want to make sure we are having devotions every morning. We try to make our Sunday morning worship services at all costs (even if we make it late). We even tithe to our local churches *exactly* 10 percent. We are keeping our fingers on the "pulse" of our Christianity.

But the real measure of our walk with Christ is whether we are keeping one foot in front of the other, walking with Him and talking with Him, believing by faith that He will help us finish the race that He asked us to run. "Being confident of this, that he who began a good work in you will carry it on to completion until the day of Christ Jesus" (Philippians 1:6).

The real measure of our relationship with Christ and our faith in Christ is our ability to act based on what we know. It's the ability to stick with it even when we can't see our way. Faith is learning how to hear His voice clearly along the way as we grow in the art of praying without ceasing (1 Thessalonians 5:17). In a way faith is not confined to a certain time of day but is like air in that we need it throughout our day to sustain us. The journey of a kingdom woman is for the woman who is willing to learn the value of getting to know Christ along the path of faith rather than focusing on the path itself.

The real measure of our walk with Christ is how much of Him we "inhale" and receive deeply within our souls until His glorious resurrection power is seeping through our pores—"I have been crucified with Christ and I no longer live, but Christ lives in me. The life I live in the body, I live by faith in the Son of God, who loved me and gave himself for me" (Galatians 2:20).

The challenge of this walk of faith is to make sure that our focus is in the right place. Although the "pulse," or indicators, that Christians are accustomed to looking at are real and do provide a gauge of what is going on inside of a person, they are *not* the end-all.

We have a God and Savior who wants us to *walk* with *Him*. He wants a relationship that transcends measurements and benchmarks. He wants us to *know* Him. Isn't that something?

I've seen many runners take a towel and cover up the treadmill dashboard that reveals the distance run, time remaining, and calories burned. Why? Because they don't want to focus on their stats; they want to enjoy the run.

My hope for my daughter was that she would not focus so much on the mechanics of the run or the requirements of the run, but that she would just run the race, knowing that all of those other things would fall into place as long as she put one foot in front of the other.

That is also my hope for you!

In life some paths lead us to where we want to go, and some paths lead us away from where we want to end up. Some roads are smooth, some are rocky, some are slippery, and some will get us stuck. I've personally traveled along paths that were painful and paths that brought me so much joy I felt I would burst.

Every now and then I've traveled a path that lasted for a brief moment, or one that flat-out exhausted me because it seemed to have no end. There have been paths lined with beauty and some lined with sights I hope to never see again. I've trodden along trails that have taken me to dead ends, and some that have led me to places I could have never imagined.

What have I learned?

The only way to live is to choose a path and follow it. Simply put: Choose to walk the path God has placed in front of you, and put one foot in front of the other. Sometimes, we don't know what our paths hold; in fact, most times we have no idea what our journeys will bring. These are the pathways with a direction and end you cannot see. The way ahead may seem blurry, but you know deep within you that God has asked you to travel this path.

> *The way ahead may seem blurry, but you know deep within you that God has asked you to travel this path.*

God always asks us to walk the pathway of faith. I can gaze at that path all I want from a distance. It is only when I choose to walk that path, to take in all the sights and sounds, to experience the journey step by step, stride by stride, that I experience my life in its entirety. It is only when I step out in faith that I am able to reach a destination that only God knew was there all along, but I could not see myself.

When walking these paths, I pray:

Lord, help me not just be a hearer but a doer.

Help me not to be a gazer but a walker.

Keep me from standing on the precipice of my life.

Hold my hand and help me to leave footprints along the paths You lead me to.

Lord, help me to boldly walk the paths set before me.

Help me to live the life You have given me fully, completely, and abundantly.

Let me experience the power provided through the life of Jesus Christ living in me.

Lord, let me live my life in such a way,

with such endurance,

with such commitment,

and with such vigor,

that when You tell me to take a foreign path with a destination I cannot predict,

I will be ready to do it boldly—knowing that You are with me along the way, that I am not alone, and that You only set me on a path of unknowing because You want me to grow in the walk and take me to a greater place through the journey.

What is your prayer? What are your concerns or hesitations? Whatever your anxieties or apprehensions, fears or trepidations, follow the instructions that the Father has given you in His Word to the path that He has for you. Walk or run in the direction He points you. Put one foot in front of the other and follow the pathway of faith.

Zipporah

The Bible is full of women whom God asked to walk a pathway of faith just as Chrystal has described. In fact, as I pored over the Scriptures looking for just the right stories to pull out to demonstrate women of faith, I came across so many women that I had to pick and choose. There aren't enough pages in this book to include each one of them, but I want us to look at a few more powerful stories. One woman acted in faith despite following a husband, Moses, who was making God mad. If you know what Zipporah must have felt like, just make sure your "amen" right now is not so loud that your husband can hear you.

Not a lot is known about Zipporah. We do know that she was of African descent. She was the daughter of a man named Jethro, who held the respected position as the priest of Midian. We also know that Zipporah married Moses after he had fled Egypt, and that their interracial marriage had been the cause of some contention in Moses' biological family (Numbers 12).

Zipporah was a proselyte to the faith. She believed in the one true God— Moses' God. And she demonstrated her fear of God and faith in Him at a time when Moses seemed to lack faith.

Moses had been instructed to circumcise his firstborn son as a demonstration of his commitment to God's covenant. The covenant was the unique agreement God had set up between Himself and His followers, the Israelites. It was the father's responsibility, according to the culture and tradition, to raise his family in the faith and to teach them to carry out the various symbolic acts and demonstrations of the faith.

God had instructed Moses that He had a big job for Moses to do. Moses was supposed to go tell Pharaoh that the judgment of God was about to come: "Then say to Pharaoh, 'This is what the LORD says: Israel is my firstborn son' " (Exodus 4:22). The firstborn son was the son of privilege and honor. God was making that point clear to Pharaoh in that He wanted His children, the Israelites, to be let go.

Yet because Pharaoh refused to let Israel go, God said, "But you refused to let him go; so I will kill your firstborn son" (Exodus 4:23). It was a high price to pay for Pharaoh's rebellion against God.

God had clearly told Moses that this was the message for him to relay. However, then Moses' problem arose: "At a lodging place on the way, the LORD met Moses and was about to kill him" (verse 24).

This is the same Moses for whom God had earlier said He had great plans. This is the same Moses God had chosen to be His leader and His mouthpiece. And yet now God was seeking to put Moses to death. That is a great turn of events if ever there was one. We know why this great reversal occurred because of what Zipporah did next. "Zipporah took a flint knife, cut off her son's foreskin and touched Moses' feet with it" (verse 25).

She did what Moses had failed to do.

She found the courage to carry out what Moses could not.

When Moses was lacking as the spiritual leader in his home, Zipporah rose up in faith and stood in the gap. Moses had failed to bring his firstborn son into the covenant with God. So Zipporah took the matter into her own hands because she feared God.

Zipporah knew that God's judgment was on her husband. So she did what many women have done over the ages. She interposed herself between God's judgment and the person who was to be judged. Interposition is when you act in obedience in an attempt to deflect God's judgment intended for someone else.

Many women have interposed themselves as an act of faith on behalf of someone else—perhaps a wayward child or even a spouse. They have diverted the judgment of God and in fact brought about blessing instead.

Zipporah's act of faith didn't come without some frustration. "But Zipporah took a flint knife, cut off her son's foreskin and touched Moses' feet with it. 'Surely you are a bridegroom of blood to me,' she said" (verse 25). She was upset. It had come on her shoulders to take care of something of utmost spiritual importance, and she let Moses know how she felt about it. Because God's wrath was against him, Moses could have ushered in destruction on his family. Zipporah's faith was all that stood between that destruction and a future.

As a result of Zipporah's strength in faith, "the LORD let him alone" (verse 26). Zipporah's faith saved Moses' life and his family.

Many lives have been saved because of a kingdom woman's interposition where husbands and/or fathers have failed. I have seen it countless times. In various counseling scenarios, the man is clearly in the wrong spiritually, and yet God appears to be blessing the couple through one form or another because of the courage of the woman's faith. That raises questions that I often hear in counseling: What do you do if your husband is not being the leader? What if he is not taking responsibility for the spiritual direction or leadership in the home? What does it mean to be submissive in the face of his own lack of submission to God? How do you follow a parked car? The man is clearly not leading spiritually, but then again he also doesn't want you to lead. What then?

Many lives have been saved because of a kingdom woman's interposition where husbands and/or fathers have failed.

The life of Zipporah gives an answer. When it comes to a matter of obeying God—fulfilling the commandments of God—you act anyway. When it comes to a matter of principle—not preference—you submit to God. See, submission does not mean that you do nothing. Submission means that you surrender to God's revealed will because your commitment to God is greater than your commitment to your husband. Men often think that "headship" is a blank check to command their wives to do or not do whatever they want. If a wife does not do it, her husband calls her "rebellious" or "unsubmissive." But the validity of headship rests in the submission of that head, the man, underneath Jesus Christ. What men will frequently do is only quote half the verse, thereby missing out on the whole meaning. Yet Scripture outlines the definition of headship:

Now I want you to realize that the head of every man is Christ, and the head of the woman is man, and the head of Christ is God. (1 Corinthians 11:3)

The order is clear: God, Christ, man, woman. To ask a woman to submit to a man who is out of alignment under God and Christ is to ask that woman to submit to something other than God, which she should never do. Men bear a responsibility to align themselves under God before they ever ask their wives to align under them.

Over my years of meeting with struggling couples, I have found this to be a primary point of contention in that a woman will often struggle between submission to a man who is clearly not living a spiritually mature life and the teachings that come from God on how she is to live her life. If there is a choice to be made over a specific spiritual principle, the choice has to be submission to God if the man is out of alignment with God's principles.

That's why the Bible limits the word *submission*. It is not an all-inclusive submission. Scripture clearly says a wife is to be submissive to her husband "as to the Lord" (Ephesians 5:22). In other words, there is a higher commitment than to your husband, and that commitment is to God. So anyone who tries to tell you that submission means you are to do whatever your husband says whether or not God agrees, that person is using the term incorrectly. Unfortunately, it is one of the most misused and abused principles in Christian homes today, and often one of the major causes leading to a breakdown of home life.

Zipporah honored Moses by honoring God. As a result of her faith, her family was saved.

Rahab

Another woman who interposed herself on behalf of her home is Rahab. Judging by her name alone, Rahab did not come from a family who believed in the one true God. Rahab's name starts with the word *Ra*. Ra is the name of a false god representing the sun, or creative powers. Rahab came from the people group known as Canaanites. Raised in a pagan environment, Rahab had grown up to choose a lifestyle of indignity. Rahab was a harlot. Some people might have called her a prostitute or a whore. Some may have referred to her as a hussy, an escort, a hooker, or ho. However they referenced her, the titles all meant the same exact thing: Rahab made a living by servicing the sexual desires of men.

As is key in real estate, so it was key in Rahab's business: Location was everything. She had secured the prime spot of the city wall. Both travelers passing through as well as countrymen heading out could easily stop in for a minute, or ten, with Rahab. We read, "for her house was upon the town wall, and she dwelt upon the wall" (Joshua 2:15, KJV).

Maybe it was precisely because foreigners visited Rahab's place so frequently that the spies whom Joshua had sent to scope out Jericho decided to stop in and hide out at Rahab's home. Even though they tried to escape notice, the spies' presence drew the attention of the king's men. The king then sent emissaries to track them down.

Rahab then faced the decision of her lifetime. Would she risk sudden death for harboring spies—if the king's emissaries were to find out—or would she risk the potential disaster that was looming from the Israelites' God? You can tell an awful lot about people by what they do rather than by what they say. Rahab's actions revealed where her faith really was—it was in the one true God. We know this because she sent the king's emissaries off on a wild-Israelite chase while helping the spies sneak back to their waiting army.

Rahab backed up her actions with her words when she revealed why she did what she did:

> [Rahab] said to them [the spies], "I know that the LORD has given this land to you and that a great fear of you has fallen on us, so that all who live in this country are melting in fear because of you. We have heard how the LORD dried up the water of the Red Sea for you when you came out of Egypt, and what you did to Sihon and Og, the two kings of the Amorites east of the Jordan, whom you completely destroyed. When we heard of it, our hearts melted and everyone's courage failed because of you, for the LORD your God is God in heaven above and on the earth below." (Verses 9–11)

Rahab's faith controlled her feet. Her faith dictated her actions. Her faith determined what she did. She hid the spies and then told them why. She didn't stop there, though. She also told the spies that she wanted to cut a deal with them. After all, she had just saved their lives, so saving hers and her family's should be worth reciprocation:

> Now then, please swear to me by the LORD that you will show kindness
> to my family, because I have shown kindness to you. Give me a sure
> sign that you will spare the lives of my father and mother, my brothers
> and sisters, and all who belong to them, and that you will save us from
> death. (Verses 12–13)

Rahab cut a deal with God's people. She asked for kindness and reminded them that she had just dealt *kindly* with them. Because of that, she wanted them to deal *kindly* with her and her family. She used the Hebrew word *chesed*, which has since been translated as "kindly." *Chesed* didn't just mean to be nice. *Chesed* specifically meant loyalty and faithfulness.[1] Appearing more than two hundred times in the Old Testament, *chesed* specifically refers to the attitude toward an agreement or covenant. It is the word used more frequently than any other to define a covenant connection. Most of the time, it was used to describe God's covenantal covering of the people of Israel despite their unfaithfulness.

Chesed means kindness on steroids. It refers to a loyal love, whether or not the other party deserves it. Rahab knew that she had nothing in her background, history, or culture to appeal to the Israelites to have mercy on her. So she asked them to remember her one act of faith with a *chesed* covenant of kindness.

*Rahab's faith made
a hooker holy.*

As a result, Rahab's faith made a hooker holy. Not only did the spies honor her request and keep everyone safe who stayed put in her home, but Rahab also landed a spot in the Israelites' highest place of honor. She made it into the Hebrews 11 Hall of Faith. Her faith put her in the same chapter as the patriarch Abraham. She stands shoulder to shoulder with other men and women of courageous faith.

An interesting aspect of Rahab's story that often gets overlooked is how Rahab and her family survived. After all, Scripture tells us that Rahab's home was on the wall. Yet Scripture also tells us that the Israelites walked around the city once a day for six days, and on the seventh day they walked around it seven times, blew their trumpets, and shouted, and the wall collapsed (Joshua 6). Jericho's ground zero was a disaster zone.

Except for one spot. Rahab's home.

While the wall crumbled all around Rahab's family, her home remained intact. She and her family were safe. I'm sure people couldn't understand it at the time, and many probably couldn't even believe how everyone in her home made it out safely. But they did because of God's covenantal *chesed* covering.

There is an interesting true story told about ground zero at the World Trade Center in New York City. After more than a month of searching and cleaning up among the rubble and destruction, the rescue crew who had been desperately scouring the grounds in search of any life or hope came across a lone Callery pear tree still alive. Somehow, buried beneath the mound of dust, debris, concrete, and twisted metal, this tree survived.

At the time that the workers pulled it from the wreckage, it had been badly charred and had only one branch remaining. This pear tree apparently wasn't ready to go when everything around it fell down. The pear tree survived what no one thought any living organism could survive.

Fast-forward a little over a decade, and the Survivor Tree—as it has affectionately and respectfully been named along with five others from the wreckage—is now more than thirty feet high, replanted in the memorial gardens honoring the memories of those killed on 9/11.[2]

The Survivor Tree offers a reminder to us of the power of hope. It also points us to another tree that stood on a hill more than two thousand years ago in the shape of a cross. This tree and the life attached to it somehow survived the destruction surrounding it as the sins of the world came collapsing around it, sending the One who hung on it deep into the depths of the earth. Yet three days later, God raised Jesus from the dead, offering those who place their trust in Him a living hope and abundant life more powerful than anything they face.

Rahab knew the power of this hope. She knew the strength of faith. Her story is one of survival as well. After all, her house was in the wall. There were two ways that people died that day in Jericho. Either they died as a result of the wall crumbling and collapsing upon them, or they died at the hands of the Israelite army.

The spies honored Rahab's request not to harm her or her family as long as they stayed in their home on the wall. But the spies had no control over how that wall would collapse or if any portion of it would remain intact.

I would be curious to know what Rahab and her family were thinking as they felt the tremors when the Jericho wall began to shake. They had been told not to leave their home, and yet now their home threatened to bury them alive.

Some say that Rahab's faith was in hiding the spies. Yet her greater faith may have been in staying inside as the walls around her crumbled.

Imagine the temptation to run outside as the tremors, shaking, and crumbling began. Yet Rahab stayed inside because of her faith in the words of the spies—and ultimately because of her faith in God, knowing that she had been instructed that her safety was within her home.

All the army did, and could do, was walk around the wall. Nowhere does Scripture tell us that when they got to the part of the wall where Rahab lived, the army tiptoed. Rather, God collapsed the wall, all the while protecting the portion where Rahab and her family remained.

You can trust God in spite of what is happening all around you.

You may feel like everything around you is falling apart. It could seem like you are seeing tremors in your life, and the walls that were supposed to support and protect you are falling down. However, if you are where God says you are to remain, stay there. I want you to know that you can trust God in spite of what is happening all around you.

Both Zipporah and Rahab give us examples of women whose possibilities increased because of their faith. Zipporah's disobedient husband eventually led the nation of Israel out of slavery and bondage from Egypt. Rahab went on to marry a well-respected builder and architect named Salmon, who founded the city of Bethleham. (1 Chronicles 2:11–51, 54).

Neither of these women came from the lineage of Israel. Neither of them, based on their culture and surroundings, would have been recognized as having a tremendous amount of potential. We don't know about Zipporah's past, but we do know that Rahab had a checkered past. Despite all of that, God honored the faith of both women, who eventually experienced their glorious destinies.

I don't know what has happened in your life—perhaps you had a child out of wedlock or married a man who abused or misused you. Or maybe you made choices that took you outside of the will of God. Whatever the case, I do know that if you will respond in faith to the one true God, if you will honor Him with your actions despite the chaos around you, if you choose to walk the path of faith that He has called you to, even when you are unsure of the outcome, He will honor, protect, and establish you as a kingdom woman.

8

THE PRAYER OF A KINGDOM WOMAN'S FAITH

A story is told of a wonderful elderly Christian lady. She had very little money and lived in a run-down house, but she was always praising the Lord. Her only problem was with the old man next door. He was always trying to prove that there was no God.

One day, as the old man was walking by her house, he noticed the woman through an open window. She was kneeling down in prayer, so he crept over to the window to hear. She was praying, "Lord, You've always given me what I've needed. And now You know that I don't have any money, and I'm completely out of groceries, and I won't get another check for a week." She paused and then continued, "Somehow, Lord, can You get me some groceries?"

The man had heard all he needed. He crept away from the window and hurried to the grocery store. He bought milk, bread, and lunchmeat. He returned to the woman's house carrying the groceries. He set down the bag by her door, rang the doorbell, and hid beside the house. You can imagine how the woman reacted to seeing the bag of groceries. She threw her hands over her head and began praising the Lord. "Thank You, Jesus!" she shouted. "I was without food, and You provided the groceries."

About that time the old man jumped out and said, "I've got you now." She was too busy shouting "thank You" to Jesus to pay any attention, so he kept going. "I told you there was no God," the old man said. "It wasn't Jesus who gave you those groceries; it was me."

"Oh no," the woman replied. "Jesus gave me these groceries—and made the devil pay for them."

Prayer is a powerful tool in the hands of a kingdom woman. God can even use the unrighteous to answer the prayers of His own. God often acts through people, even the people you would least suspect. He does it in cooperation with humanity. And He does it in answer to our prayers.

Prayer is a powerful tool in the hands of a kingdom woman.

When Jesus decided whom to use as one of the greatest illustrations on prayer, He chose a woman. He highlighted the tenacity and strength in this one woman as a goal all of us, both men and women, ought to aim for in our relationship with God. This woman understood the power of persistence. She understood that sometimes life is unfair, and her voice might not be heard, recognized, or valued, but she had legal rights that entitled her to more than what she was receiving. Based on those rights alone, she found the courage to keep asking for what was hers.

Luke stated up front the premise of the parable Jesus told about this woman. He said at the start of the story, "Then Jesus told his disciples a parable to show them that they should always pray and not give up" (Luke 18:1). Jesus was addressing quitting, or throwing in the towel, when you feel like you can't take it anymore or your prayers aren't accomplishing what you think they should. Jesus wanted to remind each of us of the power found through the right kind of persistence. The parable refers to those times when you honestly don't know how much longer you can endure the circumstances surrounding you.

Often, people will faint when they can no longer get a deep breath or enough oxygen to their lungs. From a young age, I have struggled with asthma. My father would take me to the emergency room when I was having an asthma attack. As you may know if you have asthma, when you are under an attack, you feel like you can't get enough air. What is usually a subconscious action of breathing now comes to the forefront of your mind. Breathing becomes an intentional activity.

The same holds true for prayer. When things are going well in our lives, we say a prayer here or there without giving it much thought. But when we face struggles or difficulties, they have a way of heightening the intentionality of our prayer life. Yet when we see no improvement over time, it is easy to think that our prayers aren't making any difference, so we stop or give up. However, what Jesus illustrated through the parable of the woman before the unjust judge is that even when things don't look like they will get better, we need to maintain contact with God because prayer is to be an orientation, not a position. Tenacious prayer is a lifestyle that produces results. Prayer is more than getting on our knees or clasping our hands while closing our eyes. Prayer is an attitude of operating in conjunction with God. Prayer involves exercising our authority for heavenly intervention in our earthly affairs.

The Widow and the Judge

The parable in Luke 18 begins by informing us that in a certain city there was a judge who did not fear God or men. In other words, he did not care what anyone else thought or said about him because he was the judge. During biblical times, it was a lot like old west times in America, when a circuit judge would travel from town to town to try cases, settle disputes, or hand down verdicts.

This particular judge in the parable must have had numerous cases within his realm of authority. And over time, he had gained a reputation for being an unrighteous judge. Judges like this one were easy targets for bribes; the wealthy could always pay him off so he would rule in their favor. The widow who had a case before him most likely did not have any money or influence. She didn't stand a chance of being heard or receiving a just decision in her case. But that didn't stop her from trying.

From Genesis to Revelation, when God wants to make a point, He will often choose the lowest of the low to do so. He will often highlight the orphans or the widows because they represent the most vulnerable in society. A widow in biblical times had a number of things against her. First, there was little protection for women in that day. If a woman had no husband to stand up for her, the culture would not stand up for her.

Second, widows in biblical times were normally poor, without any significant financial resources, since most of the jobs belonged to the men. Likewise, the fact that this particular widow had to plead her own case means that she had no friends or relatives who would or could stand up for her. She was on her own. She was alone, with what must have seemed like the entire world against her.

Jesus didn't give the exact details of the case that brought her to court, but we do know that something had happened in which she had been wronged. Something had happened that needed to be addressed legally. We do know she was requesting legal protection from her opponent. She must have felt vulnerable, at risk, and scared. She needed the law to arbitrate between her and the opposition, whose aim was to harm her.

So when she didn't get the protection she was legally entitled to from the unjust judge, she decided to keep asking. She didn't quit. Someone was out to do her wrong, and she did not possess the ability, money, or power to stop him. Only the law could stop him.

Before we dig deeper into the story, I want to pause to ask if you have ever been in a situation when the people who were supposed to help you did not. Either that or they made themselves unavailable to you when you needed them the most. Have you ever felt alone and vulnerable and yet entirely convinced that what has happened to you was wrong, and perhaps even illegal? If you have ever experienced feelings like that, then you know the situation that this woman was in. She did not possess the ability to protect herself in her culture or environment. She knew that if the judge did not intervene on her behalf, then she held no other recourse for gaining her own protection, or victory over her opponent.

Have you ever been in a situation when the people who were supposed to help you did not?

However, the judge didn't care. He was unwilling to help her and was not moved by her plight. He was an unjust judge, and it did not matter to him that this woman was entitled to legal rights. Yet what Jesus pointed out through this story was that even though the judge did not possess a heart to help the woman, he did intervene on her behalf simply to get her off his back:

> For some time he refused. But finally he said to himself, "Even though I don't fear God or care about men, yet because this widow keeps bothering me, I will see that she gets justice, so that she won't eventually wear me out with her coming!" (Verses 4–5)

Essentially, the judge didn't want to be bothered anymore. He didn't want to continually have to hear about her problem. It wasn't that he cared about her situation, or even that he cared what other people or even God thought about her situation; he was just tired of hearing her complain to him about it. He figured there was one way to get this woman off his back: Give her what she asked for! So he did just that. He gave her the legal protection that was her right to have.

We know how strongly this unjust judge felt about the tenacity of this woman, because the Greek word that is translated "wear me out" means "to give a black eye."[1] The issue wasn't that she was literally going to punch the judge or give him a black eye. To give a black eye meant to ruin his reputation. Not only was the woman wearing out the unjust judge, but he also knew that if she kept coming and coming, she had the potential to ruin his name because of his refusal to fulfill his legal obligation.

Evidently, this woman was showing up in a public court and telling the judge that he was failing to do what was right. She had taken the matter a step further than her desire for legal protection. She had questioned his name, and she did it publicly. So not only to get the woman off his back but also to protect his own reputation, the judge gave the woman what rightfully belonged to her.

Jesus makes an interesting contrast between the widow and the unjust judge and us before God: "Will not God bring about justice for his chosen ones, who cry out to him day and night? Will he keep putting them off? I tell you, he will see that they get justice, and quickly. However, when the Son of Man comes, will he find faith on the earth?" (verses 7–8). Jesus made clear that if an unjust judge who did not care about God, people, justice, or the law—yet he cared enough about his own comfort and reputation—responded to this woman's plea, how much more will God—who is just, righteous, and compassionate—bring about justice for His elect.

The widow was a stranger to the judge. The elect are not strangers to God. The elect are God's chosen ones; they are His children. You and I belong to Jesus Christ and make up His elect. If an unrighteous judge will grant legal protection to a stranger in order to protect his own reputation, how much more will God bring about justice to His own children, not only for the sake of His own name, but also for the sake of those whom He loves? Jesus makes it clear—He will not delay in doing so when you seek Him as the woman sought out the judge.

Claiming Your Legal Rights

Jesus used an interesting concept in His parable that is easy to miss. He used it a few times: the concept of justice, or legal protection. The issue at hand was not whether the judge knew the woman, liked the woman, or even felt sorry for the woman. The issue on the table was the law. She needed the judge to bring the power of the law to her situation because her opponent was treating her unjustly. She needed legal intervention.

See, there is more that can get God's attention than His relationship with you, His compassion toward you, or even the sake of His name. As a child of the King, you have fallen heir to "legal rights." These "rights" exist because of the new covenant that you came into when you trusted in Jesus Christ for your salvation. The issue that you may be facing or struggling with today may be an issue of the covenant. If it is, you are free to appeal to God.

Even though the unjust judge did not care for the woman, he responded to her request and gave her what was legally hers because she kept confronting him with the law. The judges reputation was at stake, since he was not upholding the law, and ultimately he was obligated to the law.

God is a God of covenant. He is also a God of His word. He has obligated Himself to His own Word. He has tied His name and His reputation to what He has said. He is tethered to His own covenantal agreements. And because God is by nature righteous, He is committed to His own righteous standard and will operate in concert with His own covenant.

However, many believers do not understand what their "rights" are according to God's covenant. Had the widow not known what the law entitled her to, she would have had nothing to bring before the unjust judge. Yet because she knew the law and knew what he was legally obligated to give her, she was able to confidently come again and again and again to ask for what was legally hers. Her knowledge of the law gave her a basis on which to stand.

Remember when we examined the healing of the woman who had been bent over for eighteen years? After Jesus healed her, the synagogue officials became indignant because the healing took place on the Sabbath. They told Jesus that work was not to be done on the Sabbath. Jesus' reply was telling. He appealed to the woman's covenantal right, saying, "Should not this woman, a daughter of Abraham, whom Satan has kept bound for eighteen long years, be set free on the Sabbath day from what bound her?" (Luke 13:16).

See, the Sabbath law was given under Moses. However, Abraham preceded Moses. As a daughter of Abraham, this woman fell under a covenant by which God promised to bring healing to His people when the problem came from a spiritual source. We had seen earlier in her story that the woman was not bent over because of a medical condition but because of Satan. Since it was Satan who had messed up her life, then her covenantal right as a daughter of Abraham entitled her to spiritual healing and release from bondage. She had a legal relationship that transcended the Mosaic law.

Jesus knew that. However, if you do not know your legal relationship, you can't call upon your legal rights. Some of you may have problems, situations, circumstances, and messes that have gone on for a long time, and you are wondering why God hasn't come through for you yet. Because the widow knew the law and kept appealing to the judge based on the law, she received what was duly hers. If an unjust judge will submit to the law even though he does not have regard for it, think of how much more a holy and righteous God will grant what is legally yours as His child when you ask Him for it. God is bound to His Word.

Claiming your legal "rights" is not a name-it-and-claim-it approach to life where God is obligated to do whatever you want Him to do. It is, however, taking advantage of all that God says He wants to do for His people based upon what falls within the boundaries of His sovereign will. This is the approach that Moses took when he appealed to God to change His mind and not render judgment on the Israelites based on what He had promised to do for His people (Numbers 14:11–21).

Neither has God forgotten who He is or what His nature is. But while praying in alignment with His Word, we remind ourselves and pray with the power of covenantal law.

A kingdom woman knows how to pray legally.

What a kingdom woman does is more than just pray. A kingdom woman knows how to pray legally. If you are like the widow and you have no place to turn, you need to know your standing before God. When you know your "rights," then you call on God with the authority to get His attention or favor based on your legal status granted by the blood of Jesus Christ and the new covenant. The very best way to pray is to hold up the standard of His own Word.

You open your Bible to places where God has said what He will do for His children, and you pray, "God, You don't lie and You are faithful. This is what You said, and this is what I'm asking for in Jesus' name." Those kind of prayers, based on God's Word, get answered. "I tell you, He will see that they get justice, and *quickly*" (Luke 18:8).

There are some passages in Scripture that are truly promises, such as "Never will I leave you; never will I forsake you" (Hebrews 13:5). Then there are general truths that aren't ironclad promises, "When a man's ways are pleasing to the Lord, he makes even his enemies live at peace with him" (Proverbs 16:7). In either case, pray and ask God for His blessing according to His will for you in Christ Jesus.

In terms of what He has written, God is committed first and foremost to His word, to His covenant. God is not bound to what you think. He is not bound to what others think. He's not even bound to what you feel. He's not bound to your parents, your spouse, your boss, your doctor, your friends—or anything. But He is bound to His Word. That is the one thing that He is entirely committed to. If you will learn how to pray to Him according to your covenantal rights, you will see Him open doors you thought were shut, close doors on your opposition, overcome your enemies, defeat your demons, and bring you swiftly along to your destiny. You will see the King intervene on behalf of His kingdom women who pray kingdom prayers.

Chrystal's Chronicles

I needed five hundred dollars. After adding up all of my expenses and calculating the income I could bring in, I still needed five hundred dollars.

At the age of nineteen, I was a brand-new, unmarried, single mother in the middle of my sophomore year of college, and I was attempting to figure out how to make the numbers work so I could stay in school. I think I can identify completely with the widow who went to the judge. Vulnerable, at risk, and scared. Yup, that about sums up exactly how I felt.

I had done all I could do in terms of my own figuring. I'd looked for another job, cut expenses, and gone over the numbers more times than I could count. Exhausted in my own strength, I decided that my only option was to pray for a miracle.

Rights? Did I even have any rights? Did God's covenant extend to me in my situation? Could I call out to Him based on His Word and expect Him to answer me? I figured it couldn't hurt to try, so that's what I decided to try to do.

I cracked open my Bible and did what so many of us do when we need to hear a serious word from the Lord—I let the Book fall open and hoped that the word I needed to hear was on that page.

No such luck.

But I did start reading. I read on simply because I so badly wanted to hear from Him, and I was desperate to persist until I got what I needed. Eventually, I read right into the passage covering the story of David and Goliath, and I sensed that story was the one for me to stake my prayer request on.

Even after hearing that story over and over as child, I must have read it five times on this particular day. I was searching for the message in the story—my message from God. Honestly, the more I read it, the more confused I was! What was my giant? Was my giant to conquer staying in school and have faith in God's provision and His strength to finish? Or was the giant to trust God, yield to the change in my life, head home, and start fresh?

It was probably the middle of the night when I finally got up from the kitchen table and went to bed. I had read the passage over and over, prayed over and over, journaled my heart whispers on the matter—and still no clear answer.

Exhausted, I retired with empty hands.

It was only five hundred dollars. Many years later, I can look back on that one evening of my life and be amazed at how monstrous that five-hundred-dollar deficit seemed to me. If staying in college was my giant, then that dollar amount was my sword to slay it with. And I didn't have the weapon in my possession.

As the time grew closer for me to finalize my decision to return to school or stay in my hometown, I continued to ask God for the additional five hundred dollars needed to conquer the giant in front of me. I believed with my mind that the God who owned "the cattle on a thousand hills" (Psalm 50:10) could find a way to sell a couple of those cattle on my behalf. I had rehearsed many times my belief that "my God will meet all your needs according to his glorious riches in Christ Jesus" (Philippians 4:19). So like Gideon laying out his fleece, I laid out my desires before the Lord and waited for Him to answer definitively.

I will be honest and admit that prayer is still one of the hardest spiritual disciplines for me.

He answered.

At the last minute, the mail arrived with a letter addressed to me from someone I'd never met. I opened the letter and out fell a check for five hundred dollars.

No kidding. For real. Exactly five hundred dollars.

And true to form, God's blessing didn't stop there. He continued to bless me "exceeding abundantly above all that we ask or think" (Ephesians 3:20, KJV). In fact, this initial monetary gift was the first gift of many that God would send me through a precious family throughout my time in college until I graduated.

Now you are probably assuming that with an answer to a prayer of this nature, I went on to become a tried and true prayer warrior. I'm ashamed to say this is not the case. I will be honest and admit that prayer is still one of the hardest spiritual disciplines for me. While I obviously believe in the power of prayer, I still have the tendency to spend a lot of energy attempting to exert my own power in a situation before it dawns on me to access the power of God through prayer.

The world in which we live encourages us to be all, have it all, and do it all. We are told as modern women that we can be the solution and the end-all to any situation we face. We are pushed to pride ourselves in our power, make the most of our minds, and act on all opportunities that come our way. We are a product of the do-it-yourself generation, the "Just Do It" culture, and the getting-things-done philosophy. Today's woman is supposedly self-reliant, self-sufficient, and ultimately self-serving.

But the longer I live, the more God graciously nudges me in His direction, encouraging me to lay my concerns at His feet. The longer I live, the more opportunities I have to see clearly my need for the Lord's sovereign guidance and intervention. The longer I live, the greater my view of my own weaknesses and imperfections. The longer I live, the more time I have to learn that control is only an illusion and that God is the only sure source of security, solace, and surety. The longer I live, the more I come to understand that, like the widow, all I've got is God, and prayer is one of the ways I demonstrate my dependence on Him.

While crisis praying has its place, only a shallow relationship with the Father has that kind of prayer as its mainstay. I have engaged in my own fair share of emergency prayers and been blessed to know that God does answer in His sovereignty. However, I am learning as the years go by that it is my breath prayers that offer the sweetest return. Those prayers offered up to my Savior the same as I would share them with a friend are effortless and not stressful, and I am especially delighted when He answers! There is nothing better than the Father giving me a desire of the heart just because He can and because He hears me when I share my soul with Him.

Prayer is a conversation, an attitude, a lifestyle. It can take different forms—verbal or written, quiet or loud, kneeling or standing. It is the act of taking ongoing opportunities to display my trust in the ability of the Savior to hear, understand, and deliver. Purposeful vertical communication is the act of operating in faith that the God I say I believe in is present and fully active in my life. Prayer allows me to talk to my Friend.

This exchange becomes more fluid the more I understand Him, and I understand Him more as I purposefully get to know Him by reading the letter He wrote to me. It is in this interchange—me talking to Him with my mouth, my mind, or my heart, and Him talking to me through His Word, His Spirit, or that still small voice—that I can operate in complete confidence that His promises do indeed extend to me and that I can depend on Him.

Prayer is not just for emergencies or when we need a breakthrough. Prayer is the everyday miracle where the God of the universe chooses to talk with us. And in this nearly inconceivable phenomenon, we find we can "approach the throne of grace with confidence, so that we may receive mercy and find grace to help us in our time of need" (Hebrews 4:16).

Pray because you can. Pray because you should. Pray because the God you believe in is delighted, each day, to have a conversation with you.

The Conversation

The Christian life without prayer is like driving a car with an almost-empty gas tank. You drive on fumes, hoping to make it to your destination before your car sputters and dies. Similarly, many of us try to live without prayer because we think we can get away with it—that is, until we wind up broken down on the side of the road.

The reality is that many of us struggle with prayer. We read the story of the widow and the unjust judge and see how Christ states clearly that God will hear and answer our prayers. Yet we still neglect this crucial area of life. I guess it's hard to talk to someone you can't see and who doesn't answer back in an audible voice. It's hard to have faith.

> *Many of us try to live without prayer because we think we can get away with it.*

We often view prayer like the national anthem sung before a baseball game: It gets the game started, but it doesn't really have much to do with what's happening on the field. We pray when we start our day, or we'll pray here and there, but it doesn't have a large role in our daily lives.

We aren't the only believers to struggle with prayer. Jesus' disciples asked Him to teach them how to pray because they didn't know. They asked some of the same questions we do: How do we, as physical beings, communicate with the invisible God? In fact, why do we have to do it at all?

Jesus answered their questions in Matthew 6—7. Jesus introduced how we should pray as well as how we should not pray. The precautions He listed are things to watch out for, because they will ruin our prayer lives. In fact, Jesus gives us the Lord's Prayer as a pattern or model for reverent, effective communication with God.

Pray Regularly

The first thing Jesus wants you to know is that you must pray regularly. It is expected that if you are a follower of Jesus Christ—not merely a Christian but a disciple—prayer will be a regular part of your life.

Prayer is defined as "a believer's communication with God through the person of Christ and assisted by the work of the Holy Spirit." At the core of prayer is relational communication with God. There is a difference between talking and communication. When you pray, you are not talking to yourself but to a holy God. He must be on your mind, the focus of your attention and the object of your communication.

Prayer is made possible through Christ alone; the only reason we can get to God is because the blood of Christ opened a door for us. Jesus said, "I am the way and the truth and the life" (John 14:6). He is the access point. We cannot enter into the presence of a holy God as sinful people. Access must be provided through the Son. That's why we pray in Jesus' name. The Bible tells us in Hebrews 10:19–22 that we have access by the blood of Christ. His death satisfied the demands of a holy God. Hebrews 4:16 says that we may come boldly to the throne of grace and enter into His presence. We can walk right up to His throne. Confidently, we can say, "Here I am, Lord. Jesus Christ let me in."

Prayer should be a regular part of our lives because it is so critical to us. You might be asking, "Why pray?" Hebrews 11:6 puts it this way: "Without faith it is impossible to please God, because anyone who comes to him must believe that he exists and that he rewards those who earnestly seek him." Prayer is a way of expressing faith, and without faith, we cannot please God. Even if you are weak in faith, pray anyway, because calling upon God's name is an act of faith, which will, in turn, build up your faith. Go to God, even though you can't see Him physically and He doesn't talk back to you audibly. Believe He is there because the Bible promises that He is. That will build up your faith.

Pray Sincerely

When we pray, Jesus says we must also pray sincerely:

> When you pray, do not be like the hypocrites, for they love to pray
> standing in the synagogues and on the street corners to be seen by men. I
> tell you the truth, they have received their reward in full. (Matthew 6:5)

This goes along with Matthew 6:1:

> Be careful not to do your "acts of righteousness" before men, to be seen
> by them. If you do, you will have no reward from your Father in heaven.

If you pray for the applause of people, you lose the applause of heaven. If you pray to be heard by people and not to communicate with God, you are not communicating *with* God.

Eloquence in prayer may impress people, but it has no power in heaven.

Jesus made it clear in those verses that the Pharisees were not models of prayer; they were hypocrites. *Hypocrite* is a very visual word, meaning literally "to wear a mask." Just like actors who play their parts, the Pharisees prayed so that others would see their "holiness."

In Jesus' day, the Jews prayed three times a day—at 3:00 PM, 6:00 PM, and 9:00 PM. When prayer time came, the hypocrites would go to the most crowded spots in the neighborhood—the marketplaces, the street corners, anywhere that others could observe their religious piety. Jesus told His followers to do the opposite. He said not to pray as if we are onstage, using fancy words. Eloquence in prayer may impress men, but it has no power in heaven.

Pray Secretly

The third precaution that Jesus gives us concerning prayer is that we must pray secretly.

When you pray, go into your room, close the door and pray to your Father, who is unseen. Then your Father, who sees what is done in secret, will reward you. (Matthew 6:6)

Your true faith shines through when you are alone. If you spend more time trying to impress other people than you spend communicating with God in your private prayers, then your spiritual priorities are out of line.

Jesus tells us to pray in secret, but He doesn't mean we should never pray in public. Plenty of public prayers are in the Bible. For example, in 1 Timothy 2:8 Paul told the people of the church to "lift up holy hands" in collective prayer. Jesus prayed publicly as well. He was not condemning public prayer, but He was saying that if a man prays publicly, he should also have a private prayer life. It would be wrong to present a façade at church on Sundays and Wednesdays to make people believe you want to be in the Lord's presence when you haven't communicated with God or drawn near to Him all week long. What you do in secret is who you really are.

We want to hurry up and pray so we can get to . . . whatever is next on our schedules.

When Jesus commands us to pray in secret, He means that we should shut out anything and everything that could distract us from spending time with the Lord. He tells us to physically shut the door, because we are so easily distracted. God is spirit, and He doesn't often use an audible voice to communicate with His followers, so it is hard for us to truly speak and listen in faith. We must remove those distractions so God can connect with us through the Holy Spirit.

You may think it's boring to be all by yourself in a room with no noise—just you and God. But once the Spirit connects you to the solitude of His presence, you will understand what David wrote about in the Psalms: lying on his bed in God's presence and having God fill and surround him. Those are powerful times alone with the Creator.

Pray Thoughtfully

Also, when we pray, Jesus says we are to pray thoughtfully. Matthew 6:7 says, "And when you pray, do not keep on babbling like pagans, for they think they will be heard because of their many words." This precaution is convicting. When I read these words, I remember when I was a boy, my mother often asked me to pray before meals, but I hated when she asked me on the days we ate fried chicken. I would pray with my eyes open, looking for that one perfect piece of chicken that would satisfy my hunger. I would put my hands at the very edge of my plate before I ended my prayer so that I could be that much closer to snatching the best piece of chicken. I wasn't thinking about God; I was thinking about the chicken. I just had to get through the prayer and get through with God to get to that chicken. Isn't that our attitude too much of the time? We want to hurry up and pray so we can get to the meal or the meeting or whatever is next on our schedules.

So how do we break the pattern of meaningless repetition? We must increase our knowledge of the subject (God) and bring that information to influence our prayer lives. The more we know about somebody, the more we have to talk about with that person. When you learn something of God through the Scriptures or at church, allow it to influence your prayer.

Pray Specifically

Last, let's examine Matthew 7:7. Jesus said, "Ask and it will be given to you; seek and you will find; knock and the door will be opened to you." Asking demands humility because it means you must go to Him and request something. Then Jesus continued, saying,

> For everyone who asks receives; he who seeks finds; and to him who knocks, the door will be opened. Which of you, if his son asks for bread, will give him a stone? Or if he asks for a fish, will give him a snake? If you, then, though you are evil, know how to give good gifts to your children, how much more will your Father in heaven give good gifts to those who ask him! (Verses 8–11)

Fish and bread, as Jesus mentioned in these verses, were the ordinary daily diet of the Jewish person. God is concerned about the "fish" and "bread" of our daily lives—the common occurrences in our days, the feelings of our hearts, and the details of our thoughts. He doesn't just want to hear from us when we have huge problems. He wants to hear all of our concerns and praises, big and small. If you only relate to God in the large issues of life, you make Him a 911 emergency problem solver, and you will only occasionally relate to Him. But if you communicate with Him in the "fish" and "bread" moments of your life, you will follow the instruction of 1 Thessalonians 5:17 to "pray continually."

In fact, when the verse talks about someone asking for a fish or a loaf, those are both items that are legitimate daily needs. The fish and the loaf of bread indicate things that we should be expecting God to provide. God is concerned with your needs. Bring Him your ordinary requests but also trust that He can do more than you could ever expect. He is a God of both the ordinary and the extraordinary.

Praise Him when you have food on the table. Praise Him when He opens the Red Sea. Praise Him when you have clothes on your back. Praise Him when He brings water out of the stone and manna from on high. Praise Him when you have gas in your tank. Praise Him when the doctor says your illness is cured. Praise Him for that, but also praise Him because nothing went wrong today. Praise Him because He provides for your basic needs. Praise Him for the "fish" and the "bread." Praise Him for the ordinary. And guess what! He'll be there for the extraordinary.

Prayer is a multifaceted communication channel with God. When you combine it with the principles from the parable of the widow and the unjust judge—going to God based on His Word and your legal rights through the new covenant—it can also be a powerful tool used to help you live out the fullness of your destiny as a kingdom woman.

PART III

THE FRUIT OF A KINGDOM WOMAN ~ POSSIBILITIES ~

9

A KINGDOM WOMAN AND HER PERSONAL LIFE

Whenever I'm asked what my favorite quote of all time is, I always reply with the profound words of Corrie ten Boom, author of *The Hiding Place* and World War II concentration camp survivor: "There is no pit so deep that [God] is not deeper still."[1] Corrie not only understood about intense human suffering but also lived a life in which God was prioritized above all else. She was able to access His peace in the midst of unimaginable pain.

Pain is often a part of the pavement on the road of faith and spiritual maturity. Not all who set off down this road travel at the same speed or reach the same destination. I believe the answer is linked to how well each woman not only embraces but also cooperates with God's formula for fruitfulness even in times of pain. His formula is found in John 15 and involves a process of pruning, abiding, and then ultimately bearing fruit.

The Process of Bearing Fruit

Jesus and His disciples sat in an upper room in Bethany sharing their last meal together before the crucifixion. On their way to town, their path led them through the valley of Kidron. Kidron was a grape grower's fantasyland, with fertile vineyards flourishing on all sides.

Perhaps as Jesus noticed the luscious grapes growing on these prolific vines, it occurred to Him to use this imagery for one of His most poignant teachings. In John 15:1–11, He said to His disciples,

> I am the true vine, and my Father is the gardener. He cuts off every branch in me that bears no fruit, while every branch that does bear fruit he prunes so that it will be even more fruitful. You are already clean because of the word I have spoken to you. Remain in me, and I will remain in you. No branch can bear fruit by itself; it must remain in the vine. Neither can you bear fruit unless you remain in me.
>
> I am the vine; you are the branches. If a man remains in me and I in him, he will bear much fruit; apart from me you can do nothing. If anyone does not remain in me, he is like a branch that is thrown away and withers; such branches are picked up, thrown into the fire and burned. If you remain in me and my words remain in you, ask whatever you wish, and it will be given you. This is to my Father's glory, that you bear much fruit, showing yourselves to be my disciples.
>
> As the Father has loved me, so have I loved you. Now remain in my love. If you obey my commands, you will remain in my love, just as I have obeyed my Father's commands and remain in his love. I have told you this so that my joy may be in you and that your joy may be complete.

Since the disciples were Jewish, they would likely have thought back to Psalm 80:8, where Israel was compared to a vine transplanted by God from Egypt to the Promised Land. There was only one problem with this relocated vine: It produced sour fruit. Instead of growing as God intended, the Jews got carried away with their own righteousness. Then along came Jesus. "Friends," He said, "I am the real thing. You may think you've seen vines before, but you haven't seen anything like Me. And then there's My Father; He's the vinedresser. He takes care of the vine." In this vineyard, we've been introduced to the vine and the vinedresser. In verse 2, Jesus turned His attention toward the branches on the vine. That's where you come in.

However, before we explore what being a branch is all about, let's give some attention to what Jesus meant when He said "every branch in me." To illustrate my point, all I need to do is refer to the institution of marriage. When you marry, you enter into an organic relationship; you and your spouse become one flesh. But, as many of us know, the fact that you have said "I do" does not automatically result in an intimate, rewarding marriage relationship. Sparks of love don't fly around your living room just because there happens to be a gold band around your finger. It is entirely possible (and all too common) to be married and miserable.

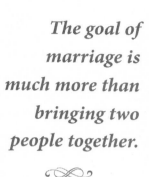

The goal of marriage is much more than bringing two people together.

The goal of marriage, then, is much more than bringing two people together. Marriage is a covenantal union designed to strengthen the capability of each partner to carry out the plan of God in his or her life. When Jesus talked about being a branch "in me," He was not alluding to those who are merely acquainted with Him. He was referring to people who abide in an intentional oneness with Him, focused on the same purpose of glorifying God and His kingdom.

Pruning

Moving from producing no fruit to producing some fruit is an important step. Still, it is just the beginning. Once you start to reflect the character of Christ, who took up residence inside you when you were saved, then God shifts into high gear. He begins pruning your branches in the hopes of producing more fruit. Pruning, for our purposes, is a matter of trimming away unwanted distractions that tend to rob the branches of the nourishment they receive from the vine.

In the parlance of the grape grower, these distractions are called *sucker shoots*, little branches that grow where the vine and branch intersect. As they grow larger, they begin to do exactly what their name suggests: They suck away the life-giving sap on its way from the vine to the branch. Before long, the branch becomes malnourished and eventually dies, all because the sucker shoot was allowed to consume what was originally intended for the branch. That's why any vinedresser worth her pruning shears will clip away those sucker shoots as soon as she discovers them. The sooner they are removed, the less damage they inflict.

All kingdom women must deal with sucker shoots of one kind or another. Some of you have friends who fit this description. Even though you start out intending to influence them, they wind up exerting more influence on you. Instead of drawing you closer to God, they lure you away, robbing you of the life-giving nourishment that results from intimate fellowship with the Father. Lifeless gadgets like televisions, iPods, and smart phones can be transformed into sucker shoots if you allow them to siphon off the time and attention you would otherwise devote to God.

When we allow our priorities to fall into disarray, we can count on some pruning. God will not stand by and watch something else suck the life out of a potentially fruitful branch. One of the interesting things about distractions is that they can be good things in and of themselves. Distractions aren't always negative things that take us away from what is good. Frequently, they are good things that take us away from what is better. The biblical story of Martha and Mary emphasizes this point clearly.

While Jesus was traveling from city to city sharing the good news, He entered a certain village where two ladies, Martha and Mary, lived. Now, even though Jesus was with His disciples—and everyone knows that if you invite thirteen preachers into your home, it means you are going to have to prepare a rather large meal—Martha took it upon herself to welcome Him and His team for dinner.

However, in the midst of preparing this enormous meal, an issue came up between the two sisters. Apparently, Mary had started out helping in the kitchen but had found her way to Jesus' feet, captivated by what He was saying. We know all of this occurred based on what Martha said to Jesus: "But Martha was distracted by all the preparations that had to be made. She came to [Jesus] and asked, 'Lord, don't you care that my sister has left me to do the work by myself? Tell her to help me!' " (Luke 10:40).

Jesus' reply to Martha gives us one of the most significant insights into our relationship with God. He said, "Martha, Martha . . . you are worried and upset about many things, but only one thing is needed. Mary has chosen what is better, and it will not be taken away from her" (verses 41–42).

In His statement, Jesus affirmed that Mary had chosen the better thing. The things that had distracted Martha were not bad things. In fact, they were good things that she was doing *for* Jesus. However, the very things Martha was doing *for* Jesus distracted her *from* Jesus.

Martha hadn't been disobeying God in her meal preparations, but she had become so involved in them that she excluded herself from time with Christ. Essentially, her calendar had become filled with cooking rather than being with her Savior.

Often when women come to me for counseling because they are struggling in their lives, it is not because of ongoing sin. Nor is it because they are bad people. Most of the time, the issues have developed because of the overabundance of good things that they are trying to accomplish simultaneously, thus leading to their priorities being out of kilter.

> *The very things Martha was doing for Jesus distracted her from Jesus.*

Another issue that often arises is the same as what happened with Martha. It is easy to blame God when things get chaotic, even if that chaos is a direct result of too much activity and misaligned priorities. Martha said, "Lord, don't you care . . . ?" Essentially, Martha was accusing God of not caring about her working so hard in the kitchen. It is important not to blame God when your own distractions are piling up and creating challenges. Martha's problem wasn't the Lord. In fact, Martha's problem wasn't even Mary.

Martha's problem was Martha.

If I could paraphrase Jesus' response, it might have gone like this: "Change your menu, Martha. If cooking a banquet is going to keep you away from Me, then a casserole will do." Not only did Martha's busy life keep her from Jesus, but it also interrupted her intimacy with her sister, Mary. Who knows how many other things or relationships Martha's preoccupied focus kept her from as well.

In your personal life as a kingdom woman, it is essential to note that in the good things of life, you should try not to lose the important things. Show me your calendar, and I will show you your priorities. How you schedule your time, as well as your resources, reveals what is truly important.

If you are not spending time cultivating your relationship with the Savior, it is not because you don't have the time. It is because you don't prioritize the relationship. Whatever is first in your life, you will find the time to do.

When our lives are deeply entangled in things that draw us away from God, He will often use that opportunity or situation to prune us. Let me point out something you have probably already noticed. Pruning hurts. There's no getting around the fact that when God starts trimming away pieces of your life, the process will be less than comfortable. The more shoots that need to be sheared, the more painful the process. Is God sensitive to your pain? Of course. But God will weigh the short-term discomfort against the long-term benefit.

I remember a certain trip to the doctor when my son Anthony was still quite young. Anthony had caught a bug and needed a shot to put him back on the road to recovery. The doctor came into the room brandishing a needle that must have looked as large as a pen to my son. "Turn around and bend over," the doctor instructed. Anthony looked at me with a petrified and pitiful look and said, "Daddy, don't let him do it. He's gonna hurt me! Daaaddy!!"

At that moment, I had to remember the long-term benefit at stake that outweighed Anthony's short-term fear and pain. Despite what my emotions were telling me, being a good father meant encouraging Anthony while he got the shot. I had to help hold down my son while the shot was delivered. Enduring the pruning process is much like facing the needle. And life is full of needles.

We have two choices before us. We can run out of the room to avoid the needles, or we can run to our heavenly Daddy. Now, our Father may keep us in the room, but that's only because He knows we need the needle.

Single Women

The story of Martha and Mary is an excellent segue into an important aspect of being a kingdom woman that applies to a great number of women today. That is the area of being a kingdom single. Nothing in the passage about Martha and Mary leads us to believe that either of these ladies was married. Typically, in biblical culture, a woman was often introduced with regard to her family status—either as *the wife of* or *the mother of.*

Yet with these two women, we never once see them connected to a husband or children, which makes the reality of Mary resting at Christ's feet more relevant than we might imagine. If Mary had needed to tend to her family and children, she might not have experienced the luxury of so much uninterrupted time in Christ's presence. Being a kingdom single has its benefits spiritually. Even Paul made note of that when he spoke of singles (we will look at that soon).

Being a Christian single is a unique and high calling.

There is often a major emphasis in the church on marriage, as there should be. Marriage is a divine institution created by God to carry out His dominion mandate on earth. So many of the church programs and even the Bible studies are aimed at married couples. However, I don't believe that enough emphasis is placed on the value and significance of singlehood.

Being a Christian single is a unique and high calling. Scripture has not ignored the subject, and in this chapter on a kingdom woman and her family, I want to make sure we do not ignore the subject either. Over the years I have encountered many singles who fall into one of two categories. Either they are frustrated as they wait for what they believe is their true purpose—a married relationship—or they jump too early into unhealthy relationships so they live dissatisfied with what they have.

Yet Paul encouraged singles to realize that they can, and should, be both satisfied and fulfilled in their higher purpose. Paul wrote frankly, "But if you do marry, you have not sinned; and if a virgin marries, she has not sinned. But those who marry will face many troubles in this life, and I want to spare you this" (1 Corinthians 7:28). Essentially, Paul equated "trouble" with marriage in this passage. He went on to explain:

> I would like you to be free from concern. An unmarried man is concerned about the Lord's affairs—how he can please the Lord. But a married man is concerned about the affairs of this world—how he can please his wife—and his interests are divided. An unmarried woman or virgin is concerned about the Lord's affairs: Her aim is to be devoted to the Lord in both body and spirit. But a married woman is concerned about the

affairs of this world—how she can please her husband. I am saying this for your own good, not to restrict you, but that you may live in a right way in undivided devotion to the Lord. (Verses 32–35)

One of the points Paul brought up is that in marriage you have now become bound to other people's expectations and needs. You can't go where you want to go as you once did as a single. You can't do everything that you want to do as you once did as a single. Everything you do must first be passed through the grid of how it intersects with meeting the needs of your family. Paul was emphasizing the freedom of singlehood. This is an area that I think a lot of singles fail to take advantage of or even enjoy to the full extent, because they are wishing that they were married. Yet if you are single, you are free.

Paul wants you to know as a single that you have a unique opportunity to maximize a heavenly perspective on earth. When you allow heaven to dictate your actions and thoughts as a single, you can become one of the most productive and significant kingdom women God has available.

The moment you become distracted by the idea of singlehood being nonfulfilling—on desiring or chasing after a mate rather than waiting on God's plan for your life (whether or not that includes a mate)—you have let your singlehood get in the way of God's purpose. In fact, you have let your singlehood get in the way of God's kingdom and your well-being because you have chosen to spend your time thinking about, feeling frustrated over, or attempting to create a way to get married. God desires you to be content where you are as a single. You have the opportunity that married women do not have to fully maximize your gifts, skills, time, treasures, and talents for the glory of God. Not only that, but you also have more time to sit at Jesus' feet as Mary did and develop an intimate relationship with the Savior.

When God made Adam, Adam didn't have a wife, but he had a purpose. He was so totally occupied with the purpose God had given him that it wasn't even Adam who noticed that he was alone and needed a helper. Scripture tells us God noticed. God made Eve and brought her to Adam. Adam didn't go looking for Eve.

Under the new covenant, there is neither male nor female in God's kingdom equation of advancing His glory on earth. As a single, you have a purpose, and God has equipped you with the power to live out your calling as a single. God will bring you a mate—as He did with Adam—if that is His will. You don't have to go looking for one. What you can do in order to live a satisfied life as a single is focus on your purpose as God's child, His kingdom daughter. And never forget, or settle for less than, your true value.

Kingdom single, you are much more valuable than you may even realize.

A man was shopping one day at an antique store where the owner, a woman, had a beautiful table for sale. The price on the table was six hundred dollars, yet the man thought he would try to get a deal, so he offered her four hundred dollars. They began having a conversation about the table, and she informed him that she wouldn't take less than the asking price for it. The man continued to ask for the discounted price, so the owner began telling him all of the unique qualities about this particular table.

Their conversation continued for some time. Then the man asked if she would be willing to take five hundred dollars. She said, "No, we've talked so much about this table, I've been reminded of its value. The price, sir, is now one thousand dollars."

Kingdom single, you are much more valuable than you may even realize. You are a child of the King; you are uniquely called and positioned to live devoted to God as one of His primary agents for advancing His purposes on earth. That is a high calling, and He will enable you to live it well. Never forget your value. Never settle for less than who you truly are.

Abiding

Several years ago, when I first preached a message on abiding to my congregation in Dallas, I wanted to illustrate how vital it is to "abide" in Christ, as the King James Version puts it in John 15. So on Saturday morning, I pulled a branch off the tree in front of my house and laid it on the porch. Then, just before I left for church on Sunday morning, I pulled a similar branch off the same tree and brought both branches with me to the pulpit. As I held them up for the congregation to see, the difference was clear. The leaves on the Sunday morning branch were still fresh and green, while the leaves on the Saturday branch were already dry and brown around the edges.

That's what happens when a branch stops "abiding" or "remaining" in the tree. It is cut off from its life source. Without being connected to the source of sap in the trunk of the tree (or vine), death begins—even though it may take several hours before it becomes apparent.

Jesus said that the key to being a fruitful, productive disciple is to abide in Him, just as a branch "abides" in a vine. As long as we do, the sap of His Spirit will continue to flow through us, and His character will burst into flowers on our branches that will ripen into luscious fruit.

The trouble with many of us is that we are not good at abiding. We fool ourselves into thinking we can survive apart from the vine. But we can't. Without abiding, it is only a matter of time before our leaves begin to wither, dry up, and turn brown, and we become unable to bear any fruit at all.

An informal study, "Obstacles to Growth Survey," reported that Christians are too busy to abide. The study gathered information from about twenty thousand Christians in nearly 140 countries. More than four in ten Christians worldwide say they "often" or "always" run from task to task. Six in ten say it is "often" or "always" true that a hectic life keeps them from going deeper in their walk with God.[2] The main problem here is in prioritizing their time to be able to abide in Christ. Abiding doesn't mean you simply pop in or pop out. To abide can be defined as "loitering" or "hanging out" with. It implies a continual and ongoing connection while in the presence of another.

Keep in mind that abiding has benefits: "If ye abide in me, and my words abide in you, ye shall ask what ye will, and it shall be done unto you" (John 15:7, KJV). This verse is often quoted by certain unscrupulous and unscriptural preachers you see on late-night TV. All you need to do is write in for this special prayer cloth or a vial of water from the Jordan River, and *presto*! your prayers (no matter how selfish and self-defeating) will be answered. But these men tend to overlook the key to this passage. It doesn't simply say to ask. It tells us to abide, and then ask: "If you remain in me and my words remain in you . . ." The world is full of people who ask but don't abide.

Psalm 37:4 says, "Delight yourself in the LORD and he will *give you the desires of your heart.*" Do you see the structure of this verse? It has the same if/ then construction we just looked at: *If* you delight yourself in the Lord, *then* He will give you the desires of your heart. *If* you abide in Him, *then* ask whatever you wish. When we delight ourselves in the Lord, His agenda becomes our own. His priorities outrank ours. We make our decisions according to His standard. His desires become our desires.

A kingdom woman who delights in the Lord may very well desire a house, a car, or some other amenity. But she will pray, "Lord, give me this house, car, or whatever so it can become Yours. Meet my need so I can build Your kingdom."

> *When we delight ourselves in the Lord, His agenda becomes our own.*

It is as though God is saying, "If you want My blessings so you can build a kingdom of your own, don't expect much. I'm only interested in answering the prayers of women who are serious about being fruitful for Me."

Bearing Fruit

"This is to my Father's glory, that you bear much fruit, showing yourselves to be my disciples" (John 15:8). As with every other facet of your life, you are to bear fruit to glorify God. The more fruitful you grow, the better you reflect the glory of God and the less you clutter your calendar with your own shortsighted agendas.

Many of the world's observatories still use giant reflecting telescopes. They work on a simple principle: An enormous curved mirror gathers light from faint, distant stars and reflects it back in crisp focus on a small eyepiece. The reflecting power of the mirror enables astronomers to view the wonders of space. Your fruitfulness as a kingdom woman makes you more reflective of God's glory and enables you to more effectively focus His light on a dark and needy world.

We've seen how vital it is to abide in Christ as the pathway to fruitfulness, but how do you actually do that? Verses 9 and 10 contain the answer: "As the Father has loved me, so have I loved you. Now remain in my love. If you obey my commands, you will remain in my love."

Remaining, or abiding, is a matter of love, not a matter of duty. Biblical love is an action, not an emotion. You abide in God's love by keeping His commandments. Without obedience, there can be no abiding. Without abiding, there can be no fruit. If you lack obedience, you might as well stop praying. If you are not obeying, you might as well get up off your knees, unfold your hands, open your eyes, and go for a walk. You can do whatever you like, but you don't need to pray. Jesus said that only those who remain in Him can expect to receive what they ask for. Yet if you are vitally connected to Jesus Christ and committed to obeying Him despite your flaws and failures, then don't hesitate to tell Him what's on your heart. It is His good pleasure to grant you whatever you wish.

You may say, "All right, Tony, I'm abiding. I have committed myself to obedience. And when I fall short of that mark, I confess my sin, repent, and get myself back into the abiding mode. I have been praying for something for the past three years, and nothing has happened. How do you make it between the time you start abiding and the time the answers show up?"

I have good news for you. If you are abiding, God has given you something to make the wait worthwhile: joy: "I have told you this so that my joy may be in you and that your joy may be complete" (verse 11). Don't be confused; joy is different from happiness. Happiness is a warm, bubbly feeling you get when things are going well. Real joy has nothing to do with how things are going. Joy is a question of your state of mind, regardless of how things are going. In fact, joy itself is called a fruit of the Spirit. Joy has to do with a God-given internal ability to cope well. It can produce peace in the midst of panic and calm in the midst of turmoil.

On the eve of His crucifixion, Jesus prayed in the garden that the cup might pass from Him. After all, there was no happiness associated with death on the cross. Jesus was willing to suffer; He was not eager for it. Many of us pray similar prayers. Your particular "cup" may be a contentious spouse, an overbearing employer, a barren womb, an empty bank account, or a chronic health problem. Just as God did not take away Jesus' cup, God doesn't take away many of our hardships. So how do we cope well? The same way that Jesus did: "For the joy set before him [He] endured the cross" (Hebrews 12:2). Jesus decided to look past the pain and see the purpose. The agony and the shame had a purpose.

If you are totally committed to this truth, you will gain insight to see beyond your circumstances and catch a glimpse of God's craftsmanship in progress. As long as you continue to seek joy from your circumstances, the best you can hope for are some fleeting moments of happiness. Some marriages, for example, are not happy ones. But they *can* be joyful. Not every job is ideal, but it can be joyful. Not every child will rise up and call you blessed, but the child-rearing experience can be a joyful one—provided that you continue to abide and obey.

Not every child will rise up and call you blessed, but the child-rearing experience can be a joyful one.

Let me give you another example. Taking a sick child to the doctor can be unnerving. The child is obviously not feeling well; that's what prompted the visit in the first place. If you also happen to be sick, the experience can be doubly stressful as your crying, restless kid squirms in the seat next to yours, anticipating what the doctor might do. That's why I was especially pleased to see that our pediatrician had set up a play area. There were blocks, puzzles, coloring books, crayons, and toy cars—plenty of activity to keep my kids interested and occupied until the doctor was ready to see us.

Friend, I know you're tired of waiting. You've been waiting for the Lord to come through and make a way out of your personal wilderness for a long time. Still, the doctor may not have called your name yet. But God has set up a room called "joy" where you can spend your time waiting with a smile on your face.

Kingdom Fruit

God doesn't take it lightly when the branches on His vine fail to yield fruit. So He will lift the branches that have fallen to the ground, nourish them, and get them up out of the dirt. But that isn't enough; He prunes the branches until they bear more fruit. Still, He is not satisfied. He will settle for nothing less than a lot of fruit.

Chrystal's Chronicles

I want to be a kingdom woman because I desire the best possible me that God had in mind when He created me. The problem is that the road to the best possible me is not always lined with roses. There have been many moments of pain and many more moments of pruning. Of course, with the passing of time and the acquisition of a few more years under my belt, I can see the blessing of hardships and trials. I can see the woman I was and the transition to the woman I am becoming. And I am learning to love it all: the past, the present, and the journey.

Even as I write this book alongside my dad, my family has had a few difficult months, which has resulted in a few difficult months for *me*. My husband, Jessie, was in the hospital three times over the course of three months. Each time there was the anxiety that accompanied a unique, unexpected emergency. Each time, there was the strain of keeping up with my children and managing my home while driving back and forth from the hospital. Each time there was the stress of thinking of the financial burden that was accruing. Each time the trip to the emergency room brought me face-to-face with the choice of trusting God and resting in His lovingkindness toward me and my family despite the circumstances.

The last visit to the hospital happened to fall on a weekend when our church had a women's event—a women's event that I was responsible for running. I came home exhausted and ready to get in the bed after a meeting at the church the Friday night before the event, only to discover that my husband was not well and needed to go to the hospital. We were up all night in the ER. I told the ladies serving with me at the church and that were available to handle things in my stead to call my cell if they had any questions. So after I'd been up all night, my phone started ringing at six o'clock in the morning. The next day, Saturday, was long. Long because we waited and waited for tests and doctors and medicine to do its thing. Long because I was on virtual duty at the women's event at my church. Long because those hospital chairs are not comfortable. And the next day I was scheduled to lead praise and worship. Now before you think I'm all holy or a supersaint, let me tell you what I was thinking: *God, are You serious?*

At this point, Jessie felt terrible that I had to miss doing ministry things and instead be with him in the hospital. I made it very clear to him that he was first and that it was important that I was with him to make sure that he was taken care of and to get information firsthand from the doctor. My husband told me that he wanted me to sing on Sunday morning. I made a run home Saturday afternoon to get things in order and prepare to be in the hospital another day. I did pack clothes for Sunday morning, just in case.

We grow up, and life happens. And we cannot control what happens to us.

Fast-forward to Sunday morning. Early in the morning the doctor told us there was nothing important going on with Jessie's treatment until the afternoon. Jessie pleaded with me to go to church.

So unbeknownst to most of my church family who saw me that Sunday morning, I got dressed for church in a hospital bathroom, left my husband napping in his hospital bed, and made my way to church. I sang at both services. I prayed in both services. I cried through both services. Then I got back in my car and drove back to the hospital.

That weekend—those months—was not the life that I envisioned when I walked down the aisle and committed myself for better or worse. But how many of us ever see the reality of the dream of the pain-free or worry-free life that we had as teenagers or young adults?

We grow up, and life happens.

And we cannot control what happens to us. Although as women we tend to think that our lives rise and fall by the choices we make, if we live long enough, we realize that we have more control of our reactions to what life throws at us than we have over the creation of the situations that life brings our way. Chuck Swindoll puts it this way:

> The longer I live, the more I realize the impact of attitude on life. Attitude, to me, is more important than facts. It is more important than the past, than education, than money, than circumstances, than failures, than successes, than what other people think or say or do. It is more important than appearance, giftedness or skill. It will make or break a company . . .

a church . . . a home. The remarkable thing is we have a choice every day regarding the attitude we will embrace for that day. We cannot change our past . . . we cannot change the fact that people will act in a certain way. We cannot change the inevitable. The only thing we can do is play on the one string we have, and that is our attitude. I am convinced that life is 10 percent what happens to me and 90 percent how I react to it. And so it is with you . . . we are in charge of our attitudes.[3]

I don't like pain, and I don't like pruning, but because I want God's best for me, I'm open to what growth requires. I try every day, while not perfectly, to have a good attitude toward those agents of change.

If you have ever sat by the bedside of a loved one in the hospital, you can understand that there is an agonizing wait for the unannounced arrival of the doctor to deliver some news about the prognosis and plan for treatment. If you have ever been a caregiver, you know that while you can't control many things, there are small things that can help your loved one get through the day. If you have ever received a diagnosis for your own health or that of someone you care for, you know the deep thump of a disappointed heart that beats loudly with questions and the unknown.

But here's what I've learned. Waiting on the doctor's report develops patience. Getting a cup of ice or propping a pillow for someone exhibits kindness. Finding calm in the midst of a sea of questions is a sign of peace. And these are all fruits of the Spirit and a life surrendered to Christ.

Pruning. Pain. Passionate pursuit of God. All three lead to bearing fruit in the life of a kingdom woman.

Don't be fooled. I'm not superwoman. I'm just one woman, living my life, learning to rest and abide in the Father's arms and to trust Him for each step I take—one step at a time. And in doing so, I find joy.

A dear friend of mine listened to me as I gave her an update on my family and specifically on my husband's health. After I poured out my heart to her, expressing the facts and my concerns, her response caught me off guard.

"Oh, Chrystal, God is giving you a wonderful testimony!"

"Huh?" I wondered.

"Well, sweetie, I'm sorry you are having to endure this difficult season, but I am so happy about the person you are going to be if you allow God to show you how to use your life lessons for His glory. God is busy at work writing your story."

My sister, God is writing your story, too. I don't know what He is allowing in your life to get it done, but I do know that He has a purpose and a plan for each and every thing that occurs in your life. And I do know that even in the darkest chapters, you can still find joy.

10

A KINGDOM WOMAN
AND HER FAMILY LIFE

While attending a marriage seminar about communication, Tom and his wife, Grace, listened to the instructor, who said, "It is essential that husbands and wives know the things that are important to each other."

He addressed the man, "Can you describe your wife's favorite flower?"

Tom leaned over, touched his wife's arm gently, and whispered, "It's Pillsbury, isn't it?"

While it's often said that marriages are made in heaven, we forget that some are thunder and lightning. Socrates supposedly remarked, "My advice to you is to get married. If you find a good spouse, you'll be happy; if not, you'll become a philosopher."

Marriage and family is frequently idealized, yet many have come to realize that it can easily turn into an ordeal when both parties do not live according to God's principles. The general statistic given for marriages that end in divorce in America is roughly 50 percent. And a large part of the 50 percent that stay together do so for reasons other than their relationship, such as convenience, finances, or kids. So based on that reality, let me ask you a question: If 50 percent of all airplanes crashed, wouldn't you be extra careful about flying?

Think about it—if you knew that one out of every two airplanes in America was going to crash, you would do a lot of careful investigation before you flew, because you wouldn't want to end up as one of those casualties. Yet roughly one out of every two marriages ends in divorce, and we still have people rushing to the altar to get married on often nothing more than emotion. And as Minnie Pearl is supposed to have quipped, they quickly find out that "marriage is a lot like a tub of hot water. Once you get in it, it isn't as hot as you thought."

A biblical understanding of the nature and purpose of the marriage covenant is essential to embracing a fruitful family environment. There is more to marriage than feelings. There is a shared calling to impact the world on behalf of God's kingdom and to glorify God in all that you do.

One of my most cherished duties while my kids were still at home was taking them to school each day. I enjoyed this because it gave us time together at the start of every day. It established an early morning routine of talking and sharing thoughts, especially because we also spent time together at breakfast.

Now that they are all adults, a day doesn't go by that I don't either see one of the kids, or several, or talk with them on the phone. I think a lot of that grew out of spending regular time at breakfast, driving to school, in the evenings doing homework, and sitting around the table at dinner. Those times established a pattern of connection that still plays out today.

One of the interesting things about driving your kids to school is that there is always a fairly elaborate system for dropping them off. Maybe you've experienced this. Anytime you have hundreds of cars and parents bottlenecked with the same purpose and the same destination but from so many directions, you need a pretty tight order to get them in and out in a minimal amount of time. There are lanes for drop-offs, walk-ins, entries, and exits.

Not only that, a police officer will often position him- or herself in the road to direct the traffic. Now, the cars are definitely stronger than the police officer. They are bigger than the police officer. They can go faster than the police officer. They can even overpower the police officer. But when the police officer merely raises his or her hand, the cars will stop. When the police officer waves his or her hand, the cars will move. The drivers do what the police officer instructs them to do. This is because the police officer has been commissioned with authority to rule over what would potentially be chaos if hundreds of cars carrying hundreds of children all tried to arrive at precisely the same time.

God Responds

Another example of chaos is 9/11. That day affected each of us differently, but what we all had in common is that it brought a foreign concept—terrorism—to the forefront of our minds. It also increased our awareness to appreciate more the time we have with our loved ones and families. It sent us on the offense, as a nation, against terrorism. Yet despite efforts to bring peace and stability to areas that lack it, terrorists continue to try to create chaos. They know that if they can keep chaos afloat, then they can limit the progress of freedom and strength in us as a country.

Satan has the same goal in mind when it comes to you living out a fully empowered life as a kingdom woman. He tries to stir things up so you cannot find order, peace, and harmony in your kingdom-woman progress. It would be similar to a number of cars in the school drop-off lanes deciding to do their own thing: Not stopping when the police officer raised his or her hand. Driving in the wrong lanes or even in the wrong direction. Failing to slow down. Any of these disruptions, even from just a small number of cars—or even if only from one car—would create disruption for everyone else trying to drop off kids.

Satan knows that if he is going to cancel your capacity to manage well, he has to disrupt order and cause confusion and dissension around you. Satan knows that whatever he can divide, he can dominate. The reason he disrupts us is because he knows that God operates in a context of unity. Satan seeks to remove God from the equation by dividing those under His rule. One of the major ways that Satan seeks to do this in a woman's life is to mess up the alignment that God has established.

When God created man and woman, He established an alignment between Himself and them as well as between genders.

Satan knows that whatever he can divide, he can dominate.

Eve was created as a counterpart, or helper, to Adam, with Adam in a position of ultimate responsibility. We know this because even though it was Eve who was deceived and ate the fruit first, it was Adam for whom God went looking in the garden to hold him accountable for their actions. God didn't say, "Adam and Eve, where are y'all?" He said, "Adam, where are *you*?"

As we saw in the first chapter, the original language describing Eve paints her as a strong partner to Adam. Eve was created to provide a *strong help* in the position of *counterpart*. She was to be a collaborator in every sense of the word. As we saw earlier, God values women so highly that He specifically tells men He will not even hear or respond to their prayers if they do not adequately show their wives honor (1 Peter 3:7). When God gave the dominion mandate to both Adam and Eve, the blessings that came from carrying out that mandate were to flow to both of them. In fact, God would not bless the man apart from the woman because the blessing was intended for both of them.

Women have been created as such an essential component of carrying out God's rule that it is no wonder Satan went to Eve first to try to disrupt that rule. He knew that if he could get to her, he would have an easier time getting to Adam. And he was right. By seeking to reverse the roles established by God, Satan introduced chaos into what was a previously peaceful garden. Essentially, Satan convinced Eve to move out of her lane. As a result, both Adam and Eve moved out of their lanes and diminished their ability to navigate (or manage) their world well. Instead of enjoying the blessings that God had promised, the very thing that had been intended as a blessing—the ground that produced fruit and foliage—now became a curse.

> *The surest way of receiving God's blessings and power in your life is to honor His alignment.*

Many today are living under the strain of chaos because they are not positioned in their prescribed lanes to enjoy all that God has intended for them. Not only does this affect them, but it affects those around them as well.

In the New Testament, this chaos that Satan seeks to introduce in believers' lives is called the "secret power of lawlessness" (2 Thessalonians 2:7). This refers to the deception that Satan brings about to create disorder and limit the power and blessings in your life. The only way to counteract Satan's schemes is to align yourself within God's prescribed order, because then you will invoke God's protection and blessing.

As a matter of fact, when you make your decisions in light of God's prescribed alignment, you will discover that He knows just how to meet your needs. Scripture tells us that God honors those who honor Him (1 Samuel 2:30), and that if you commit your way—your path, decisions, actions, and heart—to Him, He will give you the desires of your heart (Psalm 37:4–5). You won't have to try to maneuver to get them. You won't have to try to go behind, around, or over your husband to get them. The surest way of receiving God's blessings and power in your life is to honor His alignment, trusting Him with your heart because He cares for you.

Chrystal's Chronicles

Every year, I do our taxes. I majored in accounting and passed the certified public accountant (CPA) exam, so it just makes sense for me to do the taxes for our family.

It's usually an ordeal. Not because doing the taxes is hard. It's an ordeal because I have to have T-I-M-E to do it. Although in theory I could break up this monstrous project into bite-sized pieces and conquer it little by little, I prefer to dive in headfirst and hyper-focus to get it done in a huge block of time.

Typically, for three days, probably over a weekend, I convince my husband that in order for me to do our taxes, he has to assume sole responsibility for the kids so I can lock myself in a corner and give undivided attention to figuring out that special number that brings me happiness every spring—R-E-F-U-N-D.

You see, I have an ulterior motive for getting our taxes done. It means I get to spend money.

Now lest you think that I'm insensitive and work hard so that I can go and spend money on myself, give me a chance to explain. Our tax refund gives me money to spend on things for our family. We normally get the money for our homeschool curriculum from this lump sum. We also take some of the money and knock down any bills or debt that is hanging over our heads, or use it to get ahead on some of our long-term financial goals. But every now and again, I plan (sneak?) something in that is important to me for our family.

This year, this humble home manager decided that the Hurst family needed a new couch. Not just any couch. I had fallen in love with the idea of a brown-leather sectional sofa. So let me tell you a few reasons why I just knew that this was the couch for our family.

A new couch would give us some much-needed seating space in our family room. Not only do we have a larger-than-average family, but anytime we have extended family gatherings, I notice that we need additional seating. The specific couch I was eyeballing would also allow us to transition our current normal-sized couch to our game room. Ummm, let's just say that our current game room seating is "well loved." (Interpret that to mean a couch that is almost as old as my oldest child and has its innards spilling out as we speak!)

A new couch would create a friendlier atmosphere for my little ones. I envisioned a leather sectional being a perfect fit for the spills and messes that my family seems to create. How nice it would be to grab a wet cloth and wipe up the mess instead of breaking out the upholstery cleaner in hopes that I could get out a stain.

My last argument for the sensibility of a new couch was one I thought sure to win my husband over. A few months prior, for Jessie's birthday, a few family members chipped in to buy a flat-screen TV for our family room, with Jessie in mind. Although this gift was a spectacularly appreciated gift, his HDTV viewing experience was limited by the lack of good seating. I just *knew* my husband would agree with me to add leather sectional seating in our living room.

So late one evening, after slaving feverishly over our taxes in an attempt to finish before my husband went to bed, I arose victorious from my desk and almost sprinted to my husband with the final number for our tax refund. I was so excited! Not only did I have an argument; we now had the money.

I laid my case before my husband and offered him the supporting documentation. And he said no.

My face went blank. My mind doubted the ability of my ears to hear.

I went into logic mode. Men are logical, right? Well, yes, but that doesn't mean that his logic equates to mine! When logic mode didn't work, pleading mode began.

Bottom line: I lost the argument—oh, I mean *discussion*—and simply had to make up my mind to move forward and make the best of the couch we had. I also made up my mind to do my best to honor my husband's desires and drop the issue. Can someone testify with me that the hardest thing in the world for a godly woman to learn to do in her marriage is to keep her mouth closed?!

Fast-forward a few weeks. Around midday, my husband and I hopped in the car to go to a doctor's appointment together. We drove down our driveway and out to the main rural road. We made a left and drove just short of a half mile, passing the lawn of our second neighbor on the left side of the street. There on our neighbor's front lawn was a brown-leather sectional with a For Sale sign on it. The sofa I pictured in my living room had been sitting on their lawn that day—waiting for me.

> *The hardest thing in the world for a godly woman to learn to do in her marriage is to keep her mouth closed.*

By the end of the day, my new, gently-used-and-much-loved sofa sat in my living room. Delivery-charge-free. Interest-free. Hassle-free. God granted a desire of my heart.

What did I learn from this experience? God knows the desires of our hearts. And He often—but not always—honors them. I don't recall ever getting on my knees and asking God to give me a brown-leather sofa. But I do know, without a shadow of a doubt, that my loving God made sure that the sofa I wanted was conveniently available to me at a time when my own planning could not cause it to materialize.

Proverbs 10:22 says, "God's blessing makes life rich; nothing we do can improve on God" (MSG).

It is such a wonderful thing to know that God hears us even when we don't say a word. When He blesses us, He does more for us than we could ever do for ourselves.

Psalm 37:4 says, "Delight yourself in the LORD and he will give you the desires of your heart."

God hears us. He knows where we are, what we are going through, and what we desire—even if we never say a word. He loves us unconditionally and delights to illustrate His love at unexpected times and in unexpected places.

Divine Order

Chrystal's illustration reminds us of God's love and faithfulness that show up so clearly as we honor Him with our decisions and align ourselves under Him.

The primary passage written about divinely established order is found in

1 Corinthians and involves this concept of alignment. Paul highlighted this reality in the setting of an unruly Corinthian church located directly in the heart of this most profligate city of the first century.

If you have ever read 1 Corinthians, you know the church at Corinth was far from saintly. There was no order at all. In fact, everything was chaotic. Out of that atmosphere arose division, pain, and disappointment within the church. Because of the mess, Paul directed the Corinthian believers to the basic premise that underlies everything.

This might be similar to how a parent would address his or her children when they have become unruly. The parent starts with the foundation: "I'm in charge here." Paul wanted to remind the unruly church at Corinth just who was in charge—God—and how He had ordered things. So he wrote it down for them, as we saw in chapter 7:

> Follow my example, as I follow the example of Christ. . . . Now I want you to realize that the head of every man is Christ, and the head of the woman is man, and the head of Christ is God. (1 Corinthians 11:1, 3)

Paul didn't dance around it. He didn't sugarcoat it. He made it plain. When God established His order of things, He didn't hide it in some obscure location. He stated it clearly:

1. The man is the head of *a* woman.
2. Christ is the head of every man.
3. And God is the head of Christ.

Before we go on, I want to let you know that I realize that this is a sensitive topic. Trust me, I know. As I said earlier, I have counseled both men and women for thousands of hours, and the area of headship and order is often a delicate spot. So, before we go any further, I want to make this point clear: *Order has nothing to do with equality.* It has everything to do with functional effectiveness.

Jesus is equal to God. Yet while Jesus is equal to God in His being, He was not equal to God in His function on earth. Jesus said when He came to earth,

"For I have come down from heaven not to do my own will but to do the will of him who sent me" (John 6:38). He also said, "My food . . . is to do the will of him who sent me and to finish his work"
(John 4:34). What Jesus did was submit to the Father in order to carry out His function on the earth while at the same time being equal to His Father (Philippians 2:6).

> *God always works through an ordained structure.*

God always works through an ordained structure. In other words, you can't get God's involvement if you create your own structure. Satan went to Eve to flip God's order because he knew that if he could get Eve out of alignment, then both Adam and Eve would be distanced from God (Genesis 3). When roles get flipped, hell breaks loose.

I realize that sometimes people mix that up and take *function* to mean *inequality*, so they dishonor and disrespect women. The Bible knows nothing of that. That's why Scripture calls the wife a joint heir—an equal partner (1 Peter 3:7, ESV).

There is a distinction between equality of *being* and equality of *function*. Everyone doesn't play the same role. While every married woman is equal to her husband in being, she is not equal to her husband in function. When you are within your prescribed role, God is free to flow His kingdom blessings both to you and through you.

Now, I know what some of you are saying: "But Tony, what if my husband isn't a kingdom man? What if he isn't aligned under God? What do I do then?" The answer to that is simple: You align yourself under God's Word and His will while praying for your husband to get in alignment as well. As we saw earlier, Zipporah is an excellent example in Scripture of a woman whose husband, Moses, was not following God's will in a particular situation. God had instructed Moses to circumcise his sons, but Moses did not follow through with it. As a result, God's anger burned against Moses so much that God was going to kill Moses. Aware of this, Zipporah stepped in and carried out God's command.

God withheld His wrath from Moses because Moses' wife stood in the gap for him. Submission means doing so "as to the Lord" (Ephesians 5:22). When we read of the example of kingdom women in the New Testament, it says, "For this is the way the holy women of the past who put their hope in God used to make themselves beautiful. They were submissive to their own husbands" (1 Peter 3:5).

Submission acknowledges that the man is in a position of authority, but he never has absolute authority. For example, God is not asking you to submit to physical or verbal abuse. When a man seeks to harm a woman with his body or with his words, she is not called to submit to that.

What Paul wrote concerning alignment didn't just apply to women. He wrote that Christ is the head of every man. A man has to submit to Jesus Christ to open the flow of God's blessing into his home. If you are with a man who is not in alignment with God, Peter explains the power that you as a kingdom woman can have in that situation:

> Wives, in the same way be submissive to your husbands so that, if any
> of them do not believe the word, they may be won over without words
> by the behavior of their wives, when they see the purity and reverence of
> your lives. (1 Peter 3:1–2)

As a woman, you have the power to influence your husband through what you do. And as we saw in the case of Zipporah, God will take notice. That's not to say that you should never speak up. The verses are more indicative of a quiet spirit. The truth is still the truth, and all believers are called to speak the truth in love. Because each man is accountable to God, to encourage him in his role and to live in alignment with God is an appropriate thing to do.

When order is followed, it opens up the channels for God's kingdom power to flow.

One practical way you can influence your husband is by encouraging him to read *Kingdom Man* along with you. Let me be the bad guy and give him the straight truth on his role in your home. Sometimes men will listen to another man more easily than they will listen to a woman. If it's not *Kingdom Man*, encourage him to read spiritual growth books with you or to listen to biblical teaching on CD or via the Internet.

Many women have a problem with alignment because they think, *But I am smarter than my husband. I make more money than my husband. I am more educated than my husband. I have more common sense than my husband. I can't align myself underneath him.* Well, let's suppose an eighteen-wheeler is trying to merge onto the interstate. Let's also assume that there is a Kia coming down the expressway with the right-of-way. The eighteen-wheeler has to yield. Now, the eighteen-wheeler may have more size than the Kia, but the Kia has the right-of-way.

Can the driver of the eighteen-wheeler say, "Because I have more than you have, you stop on the highway and let me on"? If there is an accident, it is the eighteen-wheeler driver who is going to be at fault. Even though the truck has more weight and size, it is operating illegally.

Alignment has nothing to do with how much you bring to the table. Alignment has nothing to do with how much education, income, or fame you have. It has everything to do with God's ordained order. When order is followed, it opens up the channels for God's kingdom power to flow.

Kingdom Parenting

Volumes can be written on the area of kingdom parenting. Training up the next generation of kingdom men and women is one of the highest responsibilities that a parent can have. And while not every woman will experience what it is like to have biological children, many women who have never given birth have adopted or become spiritual mothers to relatives, church members, or neighbors. The role of parenting belongs to all of us to some degree. Single mothers in particular feel as if they face an overwhelming parenting challenge in trying to cover all of the basics that their children need. Parenting is no small role, and all of us—including me—can stand to improve how we do it. (Chrystal will look at this more closely in the next chapter.)

Scripture tells us what happens when parenting isn't applied according to kingdom principles. A curse will occur: "The young will rise up against the old, the base against the honorable" (Isaiah 3:5). The entire culture—the nation at large—suffers when children are not parented correctly. Raising kingdom kids isn't just something to do so you will have nice holidays as you get older. Raising kingdom kids is an essential component to preserving the culture from moral and spiritual decay.

Why does God want you to have children in the first place? Well, I can tell you one reason why He does not: God is not trying to create look-alikes of you. That's not His goal. God's goal for kingdom men and kingdom women raising kingdom kids is to replicate His image on earth. He wants look-alikes of Himself. The purpose of children is found in God reproducing His image in humankind all over the earth so they can advance His kingdom.

Children have a spiritual reason for existence, not just a biological, physiological, or familial reason. God wants parents to transfer a theocentric—God-centered—worldview to children. Raising kingdom kids means giving your children a kingdom perspective so they will align their decisions with His will throughout their lives. This, in turn, will bring glory to God as they reflect His rule on earth.

To raise your children with a kingdom perspective is to love them fully. By love, that doesn't mean buying them a new Xbox, clothes, and toys. There is nothing wrong with buying things for your children, but what they truly need is to learn how to be responsible, patient, hardworking, and spiritually minded. Those are the greatest love gifts you can give your children, because those gifts of love will enable them to be successful in life.

And just a note for single mothers: There will be times when you feel like you can't be everything to your children. Most likely you are working out of necessity to pay the bills, and your time is limited. However, God will help you do the best that you can to bring positive influencers into your children's lives. Regardless of your particular circumstances, your goal is still to equip them to become kingdom men or kingdom women someday.

Never underestimate the power of a kingdom woman as a mother. For example, Scripture tells us that Timothy had a God-rejecting father. He did not have a kingdom man as his dad. Yet Timothy still wound up serving God faithfully because of the teaching and encouragement of his mother and his grandmother. Teaching your children to be committed followers of Jesus Christ despite the reality that their father may not be, or those around them may not be, is one of the most important things that you can do as a mother.

Paul taught that kingdom women are to be "workers at home" (Titus 2:5, NASB). A daughter was thumbing through the family photo album one day with her father when she came across her parents' wedding pictures. She looked at her dad and said, "Daddy, when you married Mommy, is that the day you got her to come and work for you?" Now, I know what you may be thinking: *Tony, I've gone to college just like he has. In fact, I have more degrees than he has. I can make more money than he can. Why do I have to work at home when I can work better than him outside of the home?*

My answer is simple: Titus 2:3–5 makes it clear that a kingdom woman does not neglect her family for the sake of her own career. The passage doesn't say that you can't have a career—or even a very successful career. It is just that your career is not to come at the cost of caring for your home and family.

If your home is never clean because your priorities outside of the home have dominated both your time and energy, then you need to re-evaluate your priorities. As we saw earlier when we examined the woman in Proverbs 31, to take care of the home does not mean you cannot be successful elsewhere. It simply means managing the home in such a way that each member is best positioned to live for the kingdom. A kingdom woman achieves supreme significance through raising up the next generation according to God's principles and precepts.

Honoring Without Fear

In the Old Testament, we read of one kingdom woman, Sarah, whose desire for decades had been to have a child. Sarah and Abraham had been trying to have a child for years. You're familiar with the story; both were old and still had not produced a child together. Through Sarah's decision to honor God by honoring Abraham, without fear, she was blessed to conceive a child well beyond the child-bearing years.

Sarah's submission to Abraham, even in the midst of barrenness and pain, is given as one of the greatest illustrations of how a kingdom woman is to live: "like Sarah, who obeyed Abraham and called him her master. You are her daughters if you do what is right and do not give way to fear" (1 Peter 3:6).

Not only did Sarah submit to Abraham, but she also honored him as "lord." Honoring your husband is one of the greatest, most powerful things you can do as a kingdom woman. You should be your husband's biggest cheerleader. Whether you agree or disagree with him, honoring lets him know that you respect his position. And honoring him also summons the favorable attention on God.

As I explained earlier, submission doesn't mean silence or that you don't have a will and a mind. Even Jesus talked to God. He fully expressed His thoughts and feelings. Submission, however, means that you willingly come under the authority of another as long as that authority does not require you to disobey God.

If you will simply trust Him in faith, . . . God can bring your future spouse directly to you.

No man, not even your husband, has absolute authority over you. What a husband has is called *relative authority* because the moment he stops submitting himself to God, his authority over you becomes compromised. This is because you are told to obey God more than man. Submission is simply giving deference to a role when that role has also given deference to God. When you view submission that way, it takes the fear out of it.

One reason why many women today are not experiencing the miracle that they hope for in their lives is because they have chosen not to honor their husbands in their God-given roles. Yet when Sarah called Abraham "master"—essentially honoring his role in her life—she got her miracle. She became pregnant and gave birth to Isaac. Her submission led to her miracle. Sarah became the visible manifestation of what David wrote about in Psalm 128: "Your wife will be like a fruitful vine within your house" (verse 3). Not only was Sarah fruitful spiritually—after all, she wound up in the Hebrews Hall of Faith—but she was also fruitful physically, giving birth at an age when it was no longer possible. So do not let your lack of legitimate submission keep you from experiencing your miracle.

The principle of submission that applied to Sarah applies to you. And when you honor it, you will see God honor you in ways that go beyond what you can fathom. God is so good at being God that He doesn't need raw materials to create a miracle. God can call into being things that do not exist (Romans 4:17), as He did with Isaac in a barren and lifeless womb. He can take empty things and give them life. He can take a dead womb and create a miraculous intervention so it can house a heartbeat.

In fact, He can take a barren future and give it life. Or a barren career. Or a barren dream. Or a barren heart. God is a master at bringing life from what appears to be barren. If you have a barren hope, relationship, or dream, honor God as a kingdom woman and watch Him go to work on your behalf. If you are single and have been single for a long time, maybe you have given up believing that your future spouse is out there somewhere. As I said in chapter 9, you don't need to invent a way to meet your man. God is so good at what He does, if you will simply trust Him in faith and stop looking at human solutions to solve a spiritual issue, God can bring your future spouse directly to you. He can create families, careers, futures, and life where there looked to be only barrenness. Trust Him.

Tremendous freedom comes when you realize that your ultimate submission is under a caring and loving God.

A kingdom woman operates and aligns herself under the comprehensive rule of God without fear. If you will align yourself under God and honor Him in light of the distinct functions He has established within marriage and the parenting role, you can expect to experience God in unprecedented ways.

11

A KINGDOM WOMAN AND HER CHURCH

After a worship service, I enjoy greeting visitors along with those who come to our church regularly. Without fail, a line of people assembles to say hello or make some comment on the message for that day. I heard of a pastor who on one holiday saw someone whom he had seen only sporadically. So after church he said, "You come from time to time. Maybe it would be a good idea if you joined the Army of the Lord and come more regularly."

To which this lady replied, "I'm already in the Army of the Lord, Pastor."

"Well, then," Pastor asked, "how come I only see you on Christmas and Easter?"

She whispered back, "I'm in the Secret Service."

This kind of scenario happens all the time. Finding someone with a true commitment to church can be a challenge. With all that competes for time and attention, regular church attendance has fallen off of many people's list of values, let alone a meaningful church involvement.

Yet the opposite may hold true as well. You can find someone who faithfully comes to church and has done so for years, even decades, and yet her life offers only a poor reflection of the image of Jesus Christ.

Going to church doesn't make a person a Christian, or even a better Christian. A person's heart needs to be open to the process of discipleship that should be happening within the environment called the church for lasting fruit and transformation to occur.

Too often today people view the church as a hospice rather than as the hospital it was intended to be. A hospice is where people go so that they can be made comfortable while they die. They see the church as a place to feel better rather than to get better.

A hospital, on the other hand, combines staff and strategies in such a way as to make the people within it well. The focus at the hospital isn't on trying to make the patient feel good. Sometimes the doctors need to cut. Sometimes they need to administer drugs. Sometimes they need to make the person feel uncomfortable. But all of that is done to make the person healthy.

When the goal of those running the church aims at giving people a place to feel good while they die rather than a place to make them well while they live, they have missed Christ's intention for His church body. That is not the church Jesus Christ established.

When Jesus spoke of His body of believers, He referenced a strong, healthy entity that even hell itself could not prevail against. In fact the term *ecclesia* that is sometimes used in place of the word *church* in the New Testament spoke of a governing council in Greek society that legislated on behalf of the population.[1]

> *The church is intended to be much more than a social club or an entertainment venue.*

A governing council could only govern as well as the health and strength of its own members. If the members simply chose to pass the time until they passed away, looking for an enjoyable place to gather with friends, eat, and sing songs, they would not have legislated well on behalf of their community.

The church is intended to be much more than a social club or an entertainment venue. It is to be more than a place for singles to meet eligible men or women. The church is intended to be *a group of people who have been called to bring the governance of God into the relevant application and practice of humankind.*

When Jesus spoke of the church withstanding the forces of the "gates of hell" (Matthew 16:18, ESV), He chose the term for "gates" that referred to a place where legislative activities took place. The gate was where the leaders of the culture would meet to enact business and make decisions on behalf of the community.[2]

The concept of legislation for the body of Christ is reinforced by the fact that "keys" are given to the church to gain access to heaven's authority and execute it on earth (Matthew 16:19). While Jesus is positioned at the right hand of God to govern from heaven, we are also positioned with Him (Ephesians 2:6), which is why I think God will often choose what He is going to do based on what He sees the church already doing (Ephesians 3:10).

The purpose of the church reaches beyond a mere meeting place for spiritual inspiration or analysis of the culture in which it resides. The purpose of the church, *ecclesia*, is to manifest the values of heaven within the context of humankind.

These values can only be made manifest to the degree that those within the *ecclesia* reflect the values themselves. The visible demonstration of God's kingdom on earth hinges upon how many members of the body of Christ are either kingdom men or kingdom women. While the foundational context for developing kingdom women is through the nuclear family, that process is to also extend beyond the nuclear family to the local church. This is why the nurturing responsibility of the church is spoken of in feminine terms in Scripture.

The goal of the church is to transmit a biblical worldview so that women begin to think and function like Jesus Christ. Each church ought to make one of its primary priorities having a women's ministry that offers an opportunity for women to disciple women according to the Titus 2 philosophy. The church's goal is to have kingdom women encouraging and equipping other women to become kingdom women like themselves. Each church ought to focus heavily on discipleship. *Discipleship* is that "developmental process of the local church that seeks to bring Christians from spiritual infancy to spiritual maturity so they are then able to repeat the process with someone else." The fact that the culture does not offer a specific way to transmit a biblical worldview to future generations should not mean that the church shouldn't offer it. We are to reflect another culture—a kingdom culture.

Kingdom Disciples

If you want to find out what matters most to someone, read his or her last words. As you seek to be a kingdom woman, you need to know what matters most to the King, so it can matter most to you. Thankfully, you don't have to wonder about it. Just before His ascension into heaven, Jesus told us what was most important to Him:

> All authority in heaven and on earth has been given to me. Therefore go and make disciples of all nations, baptizing them in the name of the Father and of the Son and of the Holy Spirit, and teaching them to obey everything I have commanded you. And surely I am with you always, to the very end of the age. (Matthew 28:18–20)

Clearly, Christ's mandate for the church is to make disciples. That means His will for you is to become a kingdom disciple. To be a disciple of Christ means that you become like Him (Matthew 10:25). This is accomplished not just by coming to church but also by the church being a context for lives touching lives. In Paul's second letter to Timothy, he specifically said, "And the things you have heard me say in the presence of many witnesses entrust to reliable men who will also be qualified to teach others" (2:2). The Greek word translated "men" in this passage is actually *anthrōpos*, which refers to "a human being, whether male or female."[3] God expects discipleship to be done not just by men but also by women.

> *If you want to find out what matters most to someone, read his or her last words.*

Great time and effort today go into making women physically attractive. A good deal of both money and time are spent on fashion, skin, hair care, and exercise to achieve a woman's greatest beauty. Yet even the most exquisite woman on the planet loses charm and magnetism quickly if she opens her mouth and reveals an ugly interior. Far too many women are couture on the outside and bargain basement on the inside. How much time and effort are being offered today to make women spiritually attractive?

In 1979 there was an attempt to bring female representation into the US currency system with the Susan B. Anthony dollar. Unfortunately, the concept did not catch on. One of the primary reasons that this new coin failed was that the Susan B. Anthony dollar looked too much like a quarter. It had the value of a dollar but the appearance of a quarter. This is in contrast to what many women try to pull off today, which is the appearance of a dollar but the internal richness of only a quarter. This leads to confusion, disappointment, and drama in many ways simply because women have not developed within the church a system for producing quality, costly kingdom women—both inside and out.

Ladies, God doesn't want you to look like a dollar and only be a quarter. He wants your internal spiritual value to match the efforts you have made externally to be the full expression of the kingdom woman you were created to be.

In Paul's letter to Titus, he gave specific instructions to women to encourage them to live resplendently with the full glory God intended for each kingdom woman:

> Likewise, teach the older women to be reverent in the way they live, not to be slanderers or addicted to much wine, but to teach what is good. Then they can train the younger women to love their husbands and children, to be self-controlled and pure, to be busy at home, to be kind, and to be subject to their husbands, so that no one will malign the word of God. (2:3–5)

First of all, Paul specifically referenced older women. Please note that he didn't say "old" women. There is a difference. An older woman isn't necessarily an old woman. It simply means a woman who has completed the substantive part of raising her children. It could be that she has reached the stage of the empty nest. But that doesn't mean that she is no longer working or actively involved in her home, church, and community. It just means that in terms of the life cycle, the parenting days are most likely over.

Commensurate with the physical age must also be the spiritual age. Paul was speaking of the women who had gone through the spiritual lessons of life, had grown, and had overcome a number of challenging experiences. He was talking about a woman who has lived long enough to see the good, bad, and bitter that life has to offer. Yet she has also learned enough to be in a position to now transmit valuable lessons to the younger women coming behind her. She is a woman who has been exposed to and applied spiritual truth for a reasonable amount of time.

The use of your gifts in local churches is not merely incidental but is critical for the church to become what it is meant to be. Women are free to act in any aspect of the church ministry except as the final authority.

When Paul used the word *likewise*, he was pointing the reader or the listener back to what he previously said about men. Essentially, he wants the same qualities he just listed—being "temperate, worthy of respect, self-controlled, and sound in faith, in love and in endurance" (verse 2)—to also be character qualities of kingdom women. Those character qualities then manifest themselves in reverence. The word *reverent* goes hand in hand with the concept of worship. In stating that the older women are to be reverent women, Paul conjured up an image of a worshipful lifestyle. This type of woman views all of her life as a representation of a holy God.

Reverence doesn't simply show up when she's within the church walls, but her behavior highlights it outside the church in how she conducts and carries herself. A worshipful lifestyle entails an orientation that views all of life as sacred. Whether you are at church, home, work, or in your community, whatever you do, it is to the glory of God the Father and Jesus Christ, His Son.

Maybe you grew up around your mother or a grandmother who reflected that lifestyle, so you know what Paul was talking about. I did. My mother would reference anything and everything in life as connecting with God somehow. She wanted us to know that God was in the midst of everything, and that everything in our lives was somehow tied into His providence, involvement, and plan. Even if what she said or did bothered those around her, she wouldn't budge from connecting the sacred to all of life, because her life was lived in an attitude of worship. Paul indicated that spiritual maturity for a kingdom woman ought to produce a lifestyle of reverence and worship.

You will know that a woman is a kingdom woman if she knows how to hold her tongue. I see many women in the church today living in a spirit of backbiting gossip. To look more spiritual, they say that they are "concerned," "looking out" for someone's "best interest," "warning" someone, or "praying for" someone. But those around them know that they can't be "concerned" about everyone all the time; it's just a cover for a woman entangled in the sin of gossip.

Slandering and demeaning words about a third party who is not aware of the conversation is not using your tongue Godward. What it really does is alert others to your own spiritual immaturity. Using your tongue to tear down others ultimately tears down yourself. It is a neon sign of immaturity and a lack of spirituality. It doesn't matter how old you are, what position of influence you hold, or what your title may be—your tongue reveals the level of your spiritual maturity, and that's what matters when God goes looking for a kingdom woman to use for His glory and kingdom agenda.

Your tongue reveals the level of your spiritual maturity, and that's what matters when God goes looking for a kingdom woman to use.

The more mature a woman becomes, the more secure she is in herself and her relationship with God. That frees her up to build others up, help others out, and not pass along a piece of gossip when it crosses her path. For women who gossip as a way of life—I know them and you know them—all they are really demonstrating is their own spiritual lack.

Paul said that another aspect you will notice about a mature woman is that she is not enslaved to much wine (Titus 2:3). The idea here is that substances do not control her life. She doesn't have to run to the mall, to the bottle of wine, to the social club, to the antidepressants in order to infuse vibrancy into her life; her vibrancy comes from her relationship with Jesus Christ. A spiritually mature woman has made God her substance of choice.

A Teacher of What Is Good

One of the things that ought to mark a kingdom woman involves her teaching ministry. Every woman who has raised children, gone through the battles of marriage, or successfully navigated singlehood has developed life skills that need to be transmitted to those who have not yet been there and done that. Paul said that a mature woman teaches what is good (Titus 2:3). She is not just teaching stuff for the sake of teaching stuff. Neither is she teaching to promote herself, make herself look important, or be the center of attention. A mature kingdom woman teaches beneficial, helpful life lessons while making an investment in the younger women who are still learning. In the church, every older woman ought to be a teacher, and every younger woman ought to be a student.

This is especially critical today, because we have a generation of younger women who haven't even lived long enough for their lives to be as messed up as much as they are. And older, spiritually mature women are rarely to be found. Younger women need encouragers. An encourager is someone who is called alongside to help. Encouragement entails much more than classroom information, doctrine, Bible studies, and the like. Encouragement implies walking alongside someone and assisting. It is more than offering a lesson with three points on what it means to be a kingdom woman. The mature kingdom women are to bring more than just information to the table; they are to bring the experience of going through life.

There used to be a time in our culture when Christian values were transferred automatically. There was a time when women discipled women, not because there was a program and they were told they needed to disciple women, but because that was how they lived. The older women taught the younger women the basics of cooking, cleaning, working, loving, and caring for themselves and for their husbands and children. They taught priorities, values, morality, modesty, and more. Yet with the rise of autonomy, self-sufficiency, and independence came the demise of the teacher-learner atmosphere.

> *Discipleship occurs in the context of an accountable relationship.*

Often today when women meet with other women to have Bible studies or small groups, it doesn't take place in a teacher-learner atmosphere. Often everyone in the room embodies a teacher posture, and there are no learners. Or everyone merely comes to talk and have a place where they can speak about their own experiences, or someone else's, while the whole concept of discipleship is neglected.

Simply meeting together as a group of women across generational lines does not necessarily constitute discipleship. Discipleship occurs in the context of an accountable relationship. The attitude of teacher and the attitude of learner must accompany the heart of the discussion in order for life transformation to take root.

Yet somewhere on the path to autonomy, the spirit of responsibility in mentoring and leading the next generation left not only our women but also our men. The independence and self-sufficiency we so highly prize often hinder a biblical discipleship model that other cultures more naturally support and, even to this day, continue to live out organically. Many in our church culture have lost this approach to discipleship and have settled for simply gathering.

Because of this, we have become largely ineffective as a church body, even though we have multiple gatherings, numerous Bible studies, and plentiful small groups. Without practicing the model that Paul presented, the church is not effective. There must be a teacher spirit and a learner spirit present. We do not have nearly enough of that. This explains why so many women, although busy in "spiritual" things, fall so far short of being true kingdom women.

Titus 2 discipleship within the local church involves much more than ladies getting together for coffee or lunch, to be heard, to gossip, or to pass the time in a way that doesn't involve the tasks of taking care of a home and a family. Discipleship involves the ongoing translation of a life perspective by those who have lived and learned to those who are eager to learn.

One woman once told me that while she was at another nearby church, she helped to start a Titus 2 ministry. Several of the younger women signed up and were eager to take part in the process of discipleship. Yet while this church would be considered a doctrinally sound church, and even larger than your average-size church, they could not get one older, spiritually mature woman to agree to disciple the others.

This dearth in discipleship manifests itself in the large number of women who gravitate toward discipleship-based secular television. Innate within us is the desire to learn and grow. This makes such television personalities who take on a mentor-like persona extremely popular. Some examples include Oprah, Dr. Phil, the cast of *The View*, and Dr. Oz. There is a cry for discipleship among our women today. They will have a teachable spirit if placed among those whom they respect and who lead with a confident style of encouragement devoid of demeaning, belittling, or gossiping language.

The purpose of teaching is to share things that the younger women cannot see or have not seen and help them to place things in their lives in a proper order. First and foremost, Paul pointed out in Titus 2:4 that the women are to be encouraged to love their husbands. This can also apply to preparing women who are not yet married so that they will be equipped if they enter marriage.

That seems like an odd request right at the start. Why would you have to teach and encourage someone to love the person she fell madly in love with and married? It is helpful to understand the context of this passage. In biblical days, the idea of dating to marry was nonexistent. Rather, mates were often chosen for you. Similar to how Isaac and Rebekah got married soon after they saw each other, so it was in New Testament times.

That could prove to be a challenge to love a husband you didn't even know and yet were placed in an intimate relationship with. Those women who had gone through the process of learning how to love the mate they had been given were to teach the younger women the same. Based on this passage alone, we know that learning how to love biblically is possible. Biblical love is learnable when taught from the right source. Biblical love isn't based on a foundation of mutual fun, attraction, or even benefits. Biblical love means seeking the best of another in the name of God. As long as you remain the center of your universe, love will always be a struggle. *Love* can be defined as "righteously and passionately pursuing the well-being of another." There is no room for selfishness in that definition. Nor does it depend upon personal gratification.

In biblical days, the idea of dating to marry was nonexistent. Rather, mates were often chosen for you.

As a note before moving on, that doesn't mean that a woman is to remain in an abusive or controlling relationship. When a man removes himself from the headship and rule of Jesus Christ and operates in a manner that is damaging to the woman he has married, it is not love to stay and enable his behavior to continue. Often, the more loving thing to do is to stand up against abusive behavior so that he may be held accountable for it, become aware of his wrongdoing, and submit himself to God. Loving an abuser often requires leaving an abuser for a time of physical separation, because then you are no longer enabling an abuser to continue in a lifestyle of sin. When this happens, it is important to seek out the church leadership for guidance through the process of separation. At our church, we conduct church court weekly where matters like these, and others, can be looked at and governed.

Honoring God's Word

Paul also urged the kingdom women in the church to teach and encourage the younger women to be "self-controlled and pure, to be busy at home, to be kind, and to be subject to their husbands, so that no one will malign the word of God" (Titus 2:5). To be self-controlled means to make good decisions with sound judgment. This occurs only as a result of using a divine perspective.

Purity includes both actions and attitudes. Kingdom women understand that modesty does not bow to style. You can still look good and have style while dressing modestly. *Modesty* may be defined as "dressing in a way that does not draw inappropriate attention to yourself." Inappropriate attention can either be drawn by underdressing (Is it too high? Too low? Too tight?) or overdressing (Is what you are wearing opulent, extravagant, or you-centered?). Keep in mind, purity reaches beyond just clothes. Purity involves a frame of mind—what you think about, view, listen to, desire, and discuss.

We looked at the portions of this passage focusing on the management of the home in the previous chapter, so I won't go into great detail here. Basically, Paul was urging a kingdom woman to prioritize her home above other competing voices. Ladies, your home is a spiritual place. In keeping it well, you not only offer worship to God, but you also obey His high calling on your life. If you have a family—that includes being a single parent—never forget that maintaining and developing your family for God's glory is a spiritual act that God holds in high regard. Not only will He supply all of your needs to honor Him and His Word through what you do

Paul was urging a kingdom woman to prioritize her home above other competing voices.

with regard to your family, but He will also honor you as you have honored Him. God honors those who honor Him (1 Samuel 2:30).

Paul specifically tied the kingdom woman's character to a spiritual principle of honoring God's Word; a kingdom woman's lifestyle choices transcend both culture and time. In fact, in honoring God's Word through your thoughts and actions, you are bringing full-circle what Eve fell prey to in the garden. Satan deliberately questioned God's Word to Eve when he said, "Did God really say . . . ?" (Genesis 3:1). It was the very dishonoring of the Word of God that led to Eve's rebellion and sin.

In honoring God's Word, you are bringing about a reversal of the sin in the garden while inviting God's blessings and peace into your life. To follow these teachings set down by Paul is a very spiritual thing with spiritual ramifications.

Chrystal's Chronicles

I have probably read most, if not all, of the books by P. D. Eastman over and over to each of my children when they fit perfectly in my lap and when they hang on every word. *Are You My Mother?* is one of our favorites. In this book, a mother bird is watching over her egg. Right before it hatches, she goes away to find food for her soon-to-be-born baby bird. Of course, just when she is out of sight, the baby bird hatches, and the whole book tells the story of the little bird's search to find his mother—someone to nurture, teach, provide for, and protect him.

Today women of all ages and various walks of life are looking for mothers—another woman who can walk with them, disciple them, and guide them in the best ways to travel their particular road.

Just as a good physical mother operates in a capacity to care for her children, love her children, and show them the way to live a productive, responsible, and happy life, a good spiritual mother is needed to provide the same things for those in her care. Our communities are full of women who are "babies" in a way because they . . .

- are new to the Christian faith and need other women to show them the way to spiritual maturity.
- want to live as successful single women and need another woman who's "been there and done that" to lay out exactly what that means and how to do it practically.

- lack the practical knowledge of how to be good mothers to their own children and need other women to show them the ropes of godly motherhood.
- are bearing unbelievably hard loads of sickness, divorce, financial trouble, or emotional distress and need other women to care for them, love on them, listen to them, and pray with them.

Plus, in the absence of spiritual motherhood that Titus 2 says we need, we have a generation of women who are learning the world's definition of *woman* through TV, movies, magazines, and a boatload of self-help books. So women who are babies in a particular area of their lives end up lost because they can't find a mother, or they end up suffering through unnecessary struggles like the Ugly Duckling who suffered abuse and neglect before realizing he didn't belong where he was in the first place.

What does the Bible have to say about this concept of spiritual motherhood? In Genesis 3:20, "Adam named his wife Eve, because she would become the mother of all the living." In Genesis 17:15–16, "God also said to Abraham, 'As for Sarai your wife, you are no longer to call her Sarai; her name will be Sarah. I will bless her and will surely give you a son by her. I will bless her so that she will be the mother of nations; kings of peoples will come from her.' " In Genesis 24:59–60, "Rebekah [was sent] on her way. . . . And they blessed Rebekah and said to her, 'Our sister, may you increase to thousands upon thousands; may your offspring possess the gates of their enemies.' "

Based on these three verses, these three women were connected in an interesting way. All three women received a commission for fruitfulness before they ever were physically fruitful. Eve's name was based on an expectation of fruitfulness. Sarah's name was *changed* based on an expectation of fruitfulness predicated by a miracle. Rebekah received a blessing of fruitfulness at the origin of her new life as a married woman—which meant she underwent a name change.

What is significant here? Every time a woman underwent a name change or a change in identity, she also inherited a call to fruitfulness.

A funny and sometimes irritating thing for a newly married woman is the regular question she gets as soon as she ties the knot: "When are you gonna have a baby?" Why do people ask that question? It's because with the change in identity comes an expectation of fruitfulness. Romans 7:4 says, "You also died to the law through the body of Christ, that you might belong to another, to him who was raised from the dead, in order that we might bear fruit to God."

John 15:8 says, "This is to my Father's glory, that you bear much fruit, showing yourselves to be my disciples." My sister, if you are a Christian, you have a new identity, and you are called to bear fruit. And while that looks different for each one of us depending on the stage of life that God has us in, the principle is consistent with Matthew 28:19, where we are told to make disciples.

> *Just as God has designed all living things to reproduce physically, so He wants His people to reproduce spiritually.*

Imagine that we are apple trees, and we want to produce as abundant a harvest as possible. The best way to do that is to not just attempt to grow more apples but to produce more apple trees! It is to God's glory for us to do all we can to further His agenda and His kingdom. But one day each of us will no longer be on this earth. Our "apple trees" will eventually wither and die. The only way to ensure that God's vision for biblical womanhood continues is to pass it on to another woman who can continue to bear fruit and plant new seeds to grow new "trees." Just as God has designed all living things to reproduce physically, so He wants His people to reproduce spiritually.

Your season may determine the flavor of your fruit, but it should not determine the level of your fruitfulness.

Training Disciples

You know, Jesus could have easily made His earthly ministry a solo act, traveling the country alone as He preached, healed, and taught. Instead, He chose to take twelve men under His wing and train them to carry on His message after He returned to the Father. Jesus' twelve disciples became the founders of the early church, and they in turn trained others to make disciples of all nations. Jesus' planting of the gospel into the hearts of twelve men continues to bear fruit all over the world today.

So what exactly did Jesus do? What can we learn from His example?

First, Jesus spent *time* with His disciples. He was accessible. In John 1:37–39, two of

the disciples followed Jesus and wanted to know where He was staying. " 'Come,'
[Jesus] replied, 'and you will see.' So they went and saw where He was staying, and
spent that day with Him."

I know that many of us struggle with having enough time to spend with ourselves, much less other people! We are busy, tired, overworked, and stressed out.
However, we cannot allow the pace of the world to dictate the pace at which we
operate—especially if that pace gets in the way of God's mandates to us as followers of Jesus.

When I was in school, my teachers would request two things in my early years
of writing instruction: (1) Leave margin on the left and right sides of the paper, and
(2) skip a line. My teachers asked me to do both things for one reason. They wanted
room to write too! They wanted to be able to make corrections, give me sugges-
tions, and add in better ways to state my thoughts or make my point. Let me tell
you that God wants the same thing. He wants you to live in a way that leaves room
for Him to tell you how to spend your time, whom to spend time with, and how to
best express yourself in the context of engaging others. Leave margin—make room
for the activities and people whom God wants in your life.

I know what you are thinking. *What about me? What about my time?* Once again,
let's look at the life of Christ. Our Savior did
make time to withdraw and get away to be with
the Father. But the key here is that Jesus spent
the time He had available doing things that were
important to the Father. He knew He was operating on a limited amount of time, and He knew
He couldn't afford to waste even one minute
doing something that didn't matter for eternity.
We don't have that luxury either.

We cannot busy ourselves doing good things and then use those good things as an excuse for skipping God's best things.

Psalm 62:5 says, "My soul, wait thou only
upon God; for my expectation is from him"
(KJV). When we consider our time as His, God
will not only tell us how to spend it but will also provide the rest and refreshment
we need. We cannot busy ourselves doing good things and then use those good
things as an excuse for skipping God's best things. He has been clear in His Word
about what the best things are.

Second, Jesus *trained* the disciples. In Luke 11, the disciples asked Jesus to teach them to pray, and Jesus modeled what prayer should look like. For whom can you be a model? What have you learned or been through that you can teach another woman so she doesn't have to learn the hard way?

Mothers, are you training your children? Bringing up children is a purposeful and intentional job. It doesn't happen by osmosis because you send them to Sunday school. In the book *Professionalizing Motherhood,* Jill Savage challenges mothers to take the job of raising children as seriously as any work-for-pay job. She implies that, in doing so, mothers have the power to make an astounding impact on their children for the kingdom of God.

If you are a "seasoned" woman who is glad to be retired or free, that doesn't disinherit you from the same job of training and modeling for other women. What young woman are you critical of regarding her behavior, attitude, or dress? Do you model the conduct and disposition of a woman who loves Jesus? Do you have a kind word of encouragement for young women in your sphere of influence? Training and modeling are not acts of judgment or criticism but actions focused on reaching the heart of another and gently leading someone else to a higher place in Christ.

Are you a woman who has achieved success in the workplace? How do you share your wisdom and experience with others who are working to use their gifts, talents, and abilities for God's glory? What have you learned about discovering and building your strengths and maximizing your potential?

The possibilities are endless. Every woman has learned something no matter how far down the road she has gone. The question is not whether there is someone you can disciple, train, or model. You just have to stop and ask the Lord who that person is!

Who does the Lord bring to mind as you are reading this book right now? A family member, a younger woman, a friend, a child even? What connection is God asking you to make?

Last, Jesus *served* His disciples. John 13:5 tells the story of how Jesus, Son of the living God, part of the Holy Trinity, washed the feet of those who followed Him. He had no hang-ups about who He was, where He came from, what He was entitled to, or what others owed Him. He served because in doing so, He illustrated the greatest act of true maturity—the willingness to make oneself available to another. Jesus, the same Jesus who sits at the right hand of God, humbled Himself and did what He didn't have to do.

Jesus did a seemingly small thing when He washed the disciples' feet, but it was that same spirit of humble servanthood that enabled Him to bear all of our burdens on the cross. Jesus didn't bear His own burden; He was willing to bear the burden of others who didn't deserve His sacrifice. And in doing so, He pointed many people to the love of Father God.

So who are you being a spiritual mother to—especially in your local church? Where are you bringing the words of Scripture to life in your everyday activities? Every day women are being born into the church. They are new to the Christian faith, new to marriage, new to single parenting, new to being single again, new to a second career, new to motherhood, new to healthy living, new to your church. Many of them are asking, "Are you my mother?" They want to know if you will make the time to disciple them, train them, serve them, and point them toward the Lord.

You may be wondering what spiritual motherhood and Titus 2 mentoring should look like in the context of the local church. One way our church attempts to provide a platform for mentoring to take place is through small groups. Women meet twice a month for fellowship and encouragement as they discuss the application of truth based on the sermon.

Another way that we encourage spiritual connection and fellowship is through special classes geared to addressing women's needs. Some of those classes are based on a season of life like motherhood, marriage, or becoming a godly woman. Other classes are focused on healing and recovery from tough situations like addiction, emotional struggles, or debt. These are classes that while only lasting for a certain period of time provide an opportunity for women to link up with others in our body who are walking the same road they are.

> *Each kingdom woman has a ministry to another woman through the local church.*

In these classes, women share the benefits of their experience using their gifts (whether that be in hair styling, cooking, organizing, or the like) with other women. The church is a wonderful place where you can utilize the gifts God has given to you! Sometimes that might mean getting creative or discovering new ways to use your experiences and expertise in life to impact others, strengthen the church, or advance the kingdom. God has given you specific gifts to be used for His purposes within His body of believers. Using your gifts and expertise is essential to building the church.

Last, the women make time to have fun together through women's events held throughout the year. Our annual women's conference is one of those events and launches our women's ministry for the next calendar year. It is followed up with "Titus 2 Super Saturdays," where the women gather twice a year for a full day of fellowship, including a general assembly, interactive talk times, and sessions on various topics, common interests, hobbies, and seasons of life. Then they make sure to leave time for *fun!* Social outings and get-togethers help the women get to know each other and live life together, making sure that no woman at the church stands alone.

A Kingdom Woman's Ministry

Keep in mind that ministering to others and loving one another with the gifts and skills that God has given to you should extend past the church's walls. Helping children in need is a good place to start. Children living in a nuclear family today are now a minority. Having the "luxury" of living in a two-parent home is not a reality for most children. Single parents often have to work two jobs just to make ends meet, and they can't be at home as much as they'd like to be. This lack of parental mentoring can leave a gaping hole in the emotional and spiritual lives of their children.

One way that you as a kingdom woman can positively impact society is by partnering you're your church in a localized outreach to public schools. That could include mentoring, tutoring, or providing any other form of family support service. The National Church Adopt-a-School Initiative trains churches and church leaders how to carry out this localized missional model. It is a scalable approach to maximizing the gifts and skills of the body of Christ and leveraging them for the kingdom. (see The Urban Alternative appendix for more information.)

Each kingdom woman has a ministry to another woman through the local church. It's a matter of prayer and God's leading to figure out what discipleship looks like for you. Your job is to seek the Lord for His wisdom in knowing what you have received, experienced, or endured in your life that would be a blessing to someone else. If you need discipling, your job is also to pray for God to direct you to a woman who can share her life with you and help grow you up in your faith so that you can experience all of the possibilities that God has intended for your life.

12

A Kingdom Woman and Her Community

The year was 1955; the location Montgomery, Alabama. The environment reeked of racial toxicity predominantly manifested in the segregation of the Jim Crow South. Although mere inches separated row eleven from the whites-only seating area on the bus driven by James F. Blake, it represented an abyss that existed between the equality and justice experienced by white and black citizens at that time.

Sitting in row eleven was a quiet, introverted, yet determinedly strong woman named Rosa Parks. A white man boarded the bus, and the driver—a man who had previously taken Rosa's money and driven off before she could board the back entrance of the bus—sought to demean her one more time. Rosa recognized his face as he turned to tell her to get up and move so that the white man could sit down. Who could forget those eyes, steel-like and unfeeling?

Rosa had just attended a course on social and economic injustice earlier in the year, a course in which nonviolent protests had been emphasized. Yet as a lead investigator assigned to sexual-assault cases against black women by white men for the previous decade, including the infamous gang rape of Recy Taylor, Rosa knew full well what noncompliance could ultimately lead to. She had every right to seek self-preservation and move.

Even so, Rosa would later remark that the memory of the brutally slain young black boy Emmett Till at the hands of white men played prevalently in her mind when James F. Blake told her to move. And because of that, she couldn't do it—no matter what risk she took.

So Rosa Parks remained seated in row eleven.

They say that actions speak louder than words, and you can tell what someone truly believes by what he or she does. Rosa's lips never offered an explanation to the white man standing with an air of entitlement beside her, waiting to sit down. Yet the forty-two-year-old woman's actions spoke with such great volume that an entire nation couldn't help but hear.[1]

> *A kingdom woman has a destiny that extends beyond her home.*

Her simple yet profound decision to refuse to give up her seat to a white man who had demanded it, to no longer accept the indignity of second-class citizenship, and instead to proclaim both her value and rights as a child of God altered the trajectory of America forever. This one act led to the birthing and maturing of the Civil Rights Movement as we know it, improving the lives of countless individuals simply because Rosa decided to both maintain and retain her dignity.

Rosa, and her husband, Raymond, never had any biological children of their own. Yet she will forever be remembered as the mother of the Freedom Movement. Her children are legion. Her influence acute, and her legacy significant.

As a kingdom woman, you have been called to take care of yourself, support your family, raise your children, and honor your husband, but you have also been called to make a maximum impact for God's kingdom. You are not to deny the other purposes in your life, but you are not to limit yourself to them either. A kingdom woman has a destiny that extends beyond her home—the legacy you leave with your community and possibly even your nation and the world.

Esther

Just as God raised up a woman named Rosa to set in motion the single largest cultural shift in American history, God used women throughout Scripture to not only impact their communities but also to impact the nation. One of those women was Esther.

Esther was a diva. In the book bearing her name, she is described as a woman "lovely in form and features" (2:7). Her name means "star." Whatever the gene pool happened to be that brought about this kingdom woman named Esther, it definitely worked in her favor.

Yet despite Esther's intrinsic blessings, she faced a number of extrinsic obstacles. Orphaned as a young child, Esther was raised by her uncle Mordecai. Living as a minority race in a foreign land, without much money to their name, Esther and Mordecai faced insurmountable odds of ever breaking through the Persian glass ceiling.

However, Esther would break through the glass ceiling with her own Cinderella glass-slipper experience. Winning the heart of the king through a long process set up to locate the next queen, after King Xerxes had banned Queen Vashti from her role, Esther obtained the honor of being called the new queen of Persia.

To put it mildly, our girl Esther was living large.

Not long after her rise to royalty, Esther faced a dilemma. Her own people had been set up for annihilation by the evil Haman through a legal and irreversible decree that her husband, the king, had signed. Esther soon discovered, through the enlightenment of Uncle Mordecai, that she had risen to a position of power "for such a time as this" (4:14).

After Esther's initial hesitation to risk her own life on behalf of her people, Mordecai explained to her that if she did not stand up at this time, then God would raise up someone else to be the deliverer. Esther took Mordecai's words to heart, asked those around her to fast and pray for three days, and then approached the king to seek his favor, at the risk of losing her own life.

For those of you unfamiliar with the story, the king extended his golden scepter, Esther's life was preserved, and she eventually went on to win the right of her people, the Israelites, to defend themselves against the onslaught. As a result, the Israelites took up arms, not only defending themselves, but also ultimately defeating their aggressors, while the evil Haman was hung on the same gallows he had built for Mordecai.

Esther's bravery and courage, as well as her position of influence, made her a kingdom woman with whom to be reckoned. She single-handedly secured the right to safety for an entire people group.

Although this story comes from a long time ago in a kingdom far away, the principles from Esther's life are as relevant as if the events occurred today. Have you ever wondered that perhaps God has you here in His kingdom "for such a time as this"? Have you ever considered the possibilities of your own power, through Christ, to impact not only your family, church, and community, but possibly your nation as well?

Have you ever wondered that perhaps God has you here in His kingdom "for such a time as this"?

God's kingdom involves His rule, His purposes, and His agenda. In the kingdom, one overarching principle rings true: You are blessed in order to be a blessing. You are freed in order to set free. You are redeemed in order to redeem.

Maybe you have been blessed with an excellent education or a favorable physical appearance or even a good life. Whatever it is that God has given you—be it a talent, gift, or unique capacity in life—He has done it on purpose. Not so you will hoard your blessings, but so you can use the position He has given you to bring about His purposes in the lives of others around you.

Chrystal's Chronicles

The Samaritan woman was startled when Jesus spoke directly to her. And she should have been. In that day and age, Jews did not associate with Samaritans. They were the underclass, the despised, the second-rate citizens. In John 4:9, she said, "You are a Jew and I am a Samaritan woman. How can you ask me for a drink?"

Samaritans were not considered to be of "pure" ancestry. They were not considered true descendants of the Jewish patriarchs. They were believed to be a race of people who resulted from intermarriage between Hebrews and Assyrians after Assyria invaded and conquered the northern kingdom of Israel around 721 BC. They were a group of people who were considered defiled both racially and spiritually. They were thought to be unworthy, unimportant, and unvalued by those who considered themselves "true Jews" or people with a right to a sacred heritage.

The woman at the well actually had two strikes against her: She was a Samaritan, and, well, she was a woman! It was not accepted practice for a Jewish man to speak with a woman in public. Further, it is suspected that she was not well respected as a woman in her own community either.

The Samaritan woman went to draw water from the well at noon (John 4:6). This would have been the hottest part of the day, so it is implied that she went at this time to avoid going at the same time as most of the other women who would draw water from the well. She did not want to mix with people who might look down on her or ridicule her. This woman did not meet the standard for Jews. This woman didn't even meet the standards of her own community. She was an outcast.

And Jesus talked to her.

He asked her to give Him some water. He invited her into an interaction, a conversation, a discussion about a gift that was available—even for her.

Then He offered her living water. Water that would satisfy. Water that came from the man who knew about her stained life and wanted to give her a gift from God anyway.

And the Samaritan woman wanted the gift. "Sir, give me this water so that I won't get thirsty and have to keep coming here to draw water" (verse 15). She wanted this living water so badly that she was willing to let Jesus call her out on her lifestyle (verses 16–19). She desired this living water so much that she sought to understand the difference between religion and a personal relationship with Christ (verses 20–26). This woman needed living water so desperately that with eager abandon, she left her water pot at the well and ran to tell other people in her city about this man who offered her life (verses 28–30). And those in her city believed. They believed the woman branded as an outcast. First because of her word (verse 39) and later because they experienced Jesus for themselves (verse 42).

God used the woman from Samaria to impact her entire community. She had a twofold impact—evangelistically and socially. She influenced her community socially because she became the impetus to bring together two diverse racial groups that had no connection whatsoever. It was so effective that Jesus went and spent the weekend with the Samaritans. She became the gateway through which Jesus came and stayed among the people in her community. Even though she was a woman with a checkered past, God used her to influence the lives of those around her, which goes to show that God can, and will, use anyone for His kingdom purposes when that person responds to His truth.

A kingdom woman is not a perfect woman. She is a forgiven woman. She is a woman who has been loved by the Master despite her past, her weaknesses, or her struggles. She is bold. She is the woman who, because she has nothing left to lose, puts it all on the line to point others to the Giver of Life.

> *A kingdom woman is not a perfect woman. She is a forgiven woman.*

The kingdom woman does not limit herself to lines drawn by our society across racial, socioeconomic, or cultural lines. Because Jesus has reached out to her across the great chasm created by sin, she is willing to reach out to others and offer them the word of her testimony.

She is a woman who recognizes her own depravity, either because she has been on the edge of a pit, fallen into a pit, or wallowed in the mud. She is amazed that Jesus has gone out of His way to know her by name. And because she is astonished that Jesus did not think her too low or unworthy of salvation, she is grateful.

A kingdom woman is the woman who is willing to abandon her own agenda, plans, and hang-ups to act on what God says. She is willing to leave the water pot at the watering hole and take action.

My sister, the time is now. The people in your community need you now. The folks on your street need you now. The person who sits next to you at work needs you now. It's not about your perfection. God uses imperfect people. It's not about having your ducks in a row. God wants to help you line them up. It's not about being superspiritual or without sin. Jesus Christ has covered our transgressions with His blood and His sacrifice for you and me on the cross.

The time is now. There is no better time to respond to the call of God on your life than right now. You don't need to wait until your family is perfect or your salary is just right. Spiritual sainthood is not required. It matters not that your children are still little or that you have some weight to lose. Denominational divides are not a valid excuse for denying others God's love. Your upbringing is not a reason to avoid reaching out to touch someone else and share with her what you have received. The clock is ticking.

You are more than your past, the depth of your pain, or the number of your problems. You are who God says you are. You can do what God says you can do.

You can have what He says you can have.

Be bold.

The longer you hold on to your water pot in fear of how you will maintain your anonymity or self-respect, the less time you have to share your life and your story with people who need to know Jesus can save. People are dying and need you to rush into the city to tell them about what God has done in the past and what He is doing for you right now.

The Samaritan woman didn't have it all together, but she met a man who did. Jesus offered her a way to get her life together by relying on Him.

God wants to use you. Yes, *you.* Your testimony, the same testimony that you avoid and try to hide, could be the very key to someone in your community seeing Christ—His goodness, mercy, and power.

Deborah

The year was approximately 1050 BC. The location—underneath a palm tree nestled in the mountains of Ephraim, situated just between Ramah and Beth-El. It was a time when every man and woman did what was right in his or her own eyes. Humanism had taken over in the name of Baalism, while the one true God had been subsequently marginalized.

Following the courageous reigns of Joshua and the first three judges, Othniel, Ehud, and Shamgar, Israel once again turned away from following God's commands and began worshipping idols. As a result, God delivered them into the hands of the surrounding pagan nations. He raised up the secular in order to drive His people back to Him by allowing the king of Canaan, Jabin, and his evil general, Sisera, to oppress the Jews for twenty years. It is during this period of time that God appointed a woman named Deborah to serve the Israelites in a unique and special manner. Not only was Deborah raised up within Israel as the first female judge, but God also gifted her as a prophetess.

As a judge, Deborah executed decisions for disputes among the Israelites. She became known as a wise judge, and many sought her out and traveled far to meet with her under the palm tree named after her.

As a prophetess, she had the ability to discern the mind and purposes of God and communicate those to others. As her name would indicate (*Deborah* means "bee"), she was a woman who led those within her influence with sweet wisdom like honey, but she also had a deadly stinger for those who sought to subjugate her people, the Jews.

It isn't entirely known why Deborah chose the location underneath a palm tree where she settled disputes as judge. Some speculate that it is because she was a woman, and it would not have been culturally acceptable for her to meet with men behind closed doors. For whatever reason, Deborah became the highly sought out and respected prophetess and judge who rendered decisions beneath the beauty of a palm tree while also voicing the heart of God.

It was here in the outdoor air that Deborah also warned the Israelites of the consequences of worshipping idols and urged them to return to serving God. As more and more Israelites began to respond to Deborah's urgings and returned to following God, God instructed Deborah to go up against the evil Canaanite ruler and his general in battle. Then she summoned a man named Barak, the chief of the Israelite army and a Levite, and gave him this instruction:

> The LORD, the God of Israel, commands you: "Go, take with you ten thousand men of Naphtali and Zebulun and lead the way to Mount Tabor. I will lure Sisera, the commander of Jabin's army, with his chariots and his troops to the Kishon River and give him into your hands." (Judges 4:6–7)

Because Barak was of the tribe of Levi, he was also a priest. Deborah's wisdom led her to recognize that the battle against Sisera wasn't just a physical battle; it was also a spiritual battle. Deborah knew that to win a spiritual battle, it had to be fought spiritually. So she called on Barak to represent the Israelites in a priestly fashion. Within Jewish culture, women could hold high positions of leadership within government, and even within the spiritual realm, such as being a prophetess, but women were not allowed to be priests. Deborah knew that to gain the victory in a spiritual battle, it would need to be won in the heavenlies.

Yet at a time in Israelite history where there seemed to be very few men living as kingdom men, even the priest whom Deborah asked to lead the battle charge waffled under the strain of going into battle against the odds. With the

Canaanites boasting nine hundred chariots with many more soldiers than the Israelites could muster, the battle—at least on parchment—looked as if it would be won by the Canaanites. Deborah had received word from God that the victory belonged to the Israelites, so she had faith in the outcome. However, Barak did not share that same faith. He replied hesitatingly, "If you go with me, I will go; but if you don't go with me, I won't go" (verse 8). Basically, he wasn't willing to be a kingdom man.

As a result of his lack of faith, Deborah informed Barak that the honor of ultimately defeating Sisera would no longer be his, but now that honor would belong to a woman (verse 9).

> *Deborah knew that to win a spiritual battle, it had to be fought spiritually.*

Deborah did go with Barak to Kedesh, where the armies would march out for battle. When they did, God caused great confusion to come upon the Canaanites, along with powerful rains to pour down, so that eventually "all the troops of Sisera fell by the sword; not a man was left" (verse 16).

Not one was left, except, that is, for Sisera himself, who had managed to escape on foot, ending up hiding out in the tent of Heber, the Kenite and tentmaker, whose wife, Jael, had welcomed him in and promised to give him rest and refreshment.

Jael kept her promise about the refreshment, offering Sisera milk to drink. And she kept her promise about rest. She let him fall asleep. Jael then took a tent peg and drove it through Sisera's temple, thus ending the savage reign of one of the most feared Canaanite generals of all time.

A woman had led the Israelite army into battle through prophesying about their upcoming victory, and another woman had finished the job of defeating the enemy through taking the life of the evil general Sisera. Both Deborah and Jael were kingdom women whose courage enabled them to usher in an era of peace and spiritual renewal for Israel.

Through this battle, Deborah was protecting her spiritual children (the nation of Israel) from physical disaster and oppression and from the spiritual disaster of Baalism and idol worship. She ushered them into an era that included physical deliverance as well as spiritual deliverance. Out of all of the judges, only Deborah is listed as both a judge and a prophetess. She had a unique calling that resulted in victory for her people and forty years of rest for Israel.

The historic stories of both Deborah and Jael exemplify the reality that God will raise up women to advance His kingdom on earth, particularly when the men have fallen short in ruling their God-given realm well.

Similar to the legacy of Rosa Parks, while Deborah and her husband, Lappidoth, were not known for having any biological children of their own, Deborah had a formal legacy as mother of Israel (Judges 5:7).

Ladies, you have a high calling and a high purpose. God has equipped you with the power to perform tasks that are so great they have the potential to change an entire nation. Unfortunately, many women today cannot see beyond their personal lives. Maybe it's because they have become so busy and distracted doing "good" things like Martha. I'm not sure. But what I do know is that throughout Scripture, while God does make distinctions in roles and offices, He does not discriminate between male or female when revealing His truth. He empowers and calls both to advance His kingdom on earth.

God does not discriminate between male or female when revealing His truth.

On another trip to New York City with my wife, I visited Macy's. Just outside the store were windows lined with mannequins to lure passers-by to come in. On this particular day, we noticed that a number of individuals had gathered outside one of the windows. So we decided to walk down and check it out. In the window stood several well-dressed mannequins. Yet when we looked closer, it appeared that these mannequins were blinking their eyes. As we stared at them, we soon realized that these were real models posing as mannequins in an attempt to direct people's attention to the kingdom they represented—Macy's.

As the people gathering outside the window began to detect that these were live models, they started to wave their hands and make odd faces in an attempt to get the models to break their poses. Grown adults did all sorts of contortions trying to distract the mannequin models. Yet the models held firm, accomplished their purpose, and piqued the interest of numbers of people who eventually went inside, lured by the attraction. The models were able to hold firm to their purpose because they weren't distracted by the commotion. Their job was to impact the world that was passing by rather than be impacted by it.

As a kingdom woman, you represent a King from another kingdom who has put you here on earth as a preview for all that He offers and can supply. Your job is to impact your family, church, community, and world, which are passing by, rather than be impacted by them.

A number of voices seek to distract you, and many of those voices are even good, but God has given you a purpose to represent Him and His kingdom on earth.

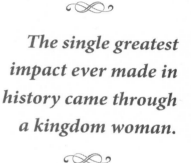

The single greatest impact ever made in history came through a kingdom woman.

As with Rosa Parks, that will require risk. As with Esther, that will require focus. As with the Samaritan woman, that will require boldness. And as with Deborah, that will require faith. Yet as with all of them, the fruit will bear a legacy resulting from the power of God's grace and worthy of Christ's name.

Ladies, please never forget that the single greatest impact ever made in history came through a kingdom woman. Mary gave birth to the Savior of the world who would offer the path for salvation to everyone who calls on His name and believes. Mary, alone and young, chose faith over fear when she boldly proclaimed regarding God's will for her life, "May it be to me as you have said" (Luke 1:38).

Let that be your kingdom proclamation as well. Then sit back and be amazed at all that God will do to you and through you.

APPENDIX

THE URBAN ALTERNATIVE

Dr. Tony Evans and the Urban Alternative (TUA) equip, empower, and unite Christians to impact individuals, families, churches, and communities to restore hope and transform lives.

TUA believes the core cause of the problems we face in our personal lives, homes, churches, and society are spiritual ones; therefore, the only way to address them is spiritually. We've tried a political, a social, an economic, and even a religious agenda. It's time for a kingdom agenda—God's visible and comprehensive rule over every area of life, because when we function as we were designed, there is a divine power that changes everything. It renews and restores as the life of Christ is made manifest within our own. As we align ourselves under Him, there is an alignment that happens from deep within—where He brings about full restoration. It is an atmosphere that revives and makes whole.

As it impacts us, it impacts others—transforming every sphere of life in which we live. When each biblical sphere of life functions in accordance with God's Word, the outcomes are evangelism, discipleship, and community impact. As we learn how to govern ourselves under God, we transform the institutions of family, church, and society from a biblically based kingdom perspective. Through Him, we are touching heaven and changing earth.

To achieve this goal, TUA uses a variety of strategies, methods, and resources for reaching and equipping as many people as possible.

Broadcast Media

Hundreds of thousands of individuals experience *The Alternative with Dr. Tony Evans* through the daily radio broadcast playing on more than 850 radio outlets and in more than eighty countries. The broadcast can also be seen on several television networks and is viewable online at TonyEvans.org.

Leadership Training

The Kingdom Agenda Pastors (KAP) provides a viable network for like-minded pastors who embrace the kingdom agenda philosophy. Pastors have the opportunity to go deeper with Dr. Tony Evans as they are given greater biblical knowledge, practical applications, and resources to impact individuals, families, churches, and communities. KAP welcomes senior and associate pastors of all churches.

The KAP Summit progressively develops church leaders to meet the demands of the twenty-first century while maintaining the gospel message and the strategic position of the church. The summit introduces intensive seminars, workshops, and resources, addressing issues affecting the community, family, leadership, organizational health, and more.

Pastors' Wives Ministry, founded by Dr. Lois Evans, provides counsel, encouragement, and spiritual resources for pastors' wives as they serve with their husbands in the ministry. A primary focus of the ministry is the KAP Summit that offers senior pastors' wives a safe place to reflect, renew, and relax, along with training in personal development, spiritual growth, and care for their emotional and physical well-being.

Community Impact

National Church Adopt-a-School Initiative (NCAASI) prepares churches across the country to impact communities by using public schools as the primary vehicle for effecting positive social change in urban youth and families. Leaders of churches, school districts, faith-based organizations, and other nonprofit organizations are equipped with the knowledge and tools to forge partnerships and build strong social-service delivery systems. This training is based on the comprehensive church-based community impact strategy conducted by Oak Cliff Bible Fellowship. It addresses such areas as economic development, education, housing, health revitalization, family renewal, and racial reconciliation.

We also assist churches in tailoring the model to meet the specific needs of their communities while simultaneously addressing the spiritual and moral frames of reference.

Resource Development

We are fostering lifelong learning partnerships with the people we serve by providing a variety of published materials. We offer booklets, Bible studies, books, CDs, and DVDs to strengthen people in their walk with God and ministry to others.

For more information, a catalog of Dr. Tony Evans's ministry resources, and a complimentary copy of Dr. Evans's devotional newsletter:

Call (800) 800-3222.

Write TUA at PO Box 4000, Dallas, TX 75208.

Or log on to TonyEvans.org.

NOTES

Introduction

1. Eleanor Roosevelt, quoted in Donald Wigal, *The Wisdom of Eleanor Roosevelt* (New York: Kensington, 2003), 86.

2. Virginia Woolf, *A Room of One's Own* (Peterborough, Ontario: Broadview Press, 2001), 59.

3. Adam Looney and Michael Greenstone, "Women in the Workforce: Is Wage Stagnation Catching Up to Them Too?" The Hamilton Project, April 2011, http://www.hamiltonproject.org/files/downloads _and_links/03_jobs_women.pdf; and Liza Mundy, "Women, Money and Power," *TIME*, March 26, 2012, http://www.time.com/time /magazine/article/0,9171,2109140,00.html?pcd=pw-op.

4. Women's Philanthropy Institute, "Boomer Women Give More to Charity, New Study Finds," Center on Philanthropy, August 22, 2012, http://www.philanthropy.iupui.edu/news/article/boomer-women- give-more-to-charity-new-study-finds.

5. Bruno Mars, "Grenade," *Doo-Wops and Hooligans* (CD), Elektra-Asylum, 2010.

6. Bryan Adams, "(Everything I Do) I Do It for You," *Robin Hood: Prince of Thieves* soundtrack, Shout Factory! 1991.

7. Percy Sledge, "When a Man Loves a Woman," *Ultimate Collection* (CD), Atlantic, 1990.

8. Jay Boice and Aaron Bycoffe, "Olympic Medal Count 2012: Standings Table of London Games Totals by Nation, Type of Medal," *The Huffington Post*, August 8, 2012, http://www.huffingtonpost .com/2012/08/08/olympic-medal-count-2012-standings_n_1756771 .html, and Timothy Rapp, "Olympic Medal Count 2012: US Women Stole the Show in London," BleachReport.com, August 13, 2012, http://bleacherreport.com/articles/1294747-olympic-medal-count- 2012-us-women-stole-the-show-in-london.

9. Sojourner Truth in a speech titled "Ain't I a Woman?" delivered in 1851 to the Women's Rights Convention, Akron, Ohio, Sojourner Truth Institute, http://www.sojournertruth.org/Library/Speeches /AintIAWoman.htm.

10. Bruce Redford, ed., *Letters of Samuel Johnson: 1731–1772*, (Princeton, NJ: Princeton University Press, 1994), 1:228.

11. *Strong's Concordance*, s.v. Hebrew 3335 *yatsar*, http://biblesuite.com /hebrew/3335.htm.

12. *Strong's Concordance*, s.v. Hebrew 1129 *banah*, http://biblesuite.com /hebrew/1129.htm.

13. Abraham Lincoln, "Speech at Lewistown, Illinois, August 17, 1858," *Lincoln Speeches* (New York: Penguin, 2012), http://books.google .com/books?id=lhmbVKFw8rQC&pg=PT8&dq=Lewiston,+I llinois+August+17,+1858&hl=en&sa=X&ei=h0z4UPu-NIeuq QGXwoGIDw&ved=0CDQQ6AEwATgK#v=onepage&q=div ine%20image&f=false.

14. *Bible Suite, Multi-Version Concordance*, s.v. *church*, http://biblesuite .com/c/church.htm.

15. *Bible Suite, Multi-Version Concordance*, s.v. *kingdom*, http://biblesuite .com/k/kingdom.htm.

16. *Strong's Concordance*, s.v. Greek 932 *basileia*, http://biblesuite.com /greek/932.htm.

17. Tony Evans, *The Kingdom Agenda* (Chicago: Moody, 2006), 27.

18. *Strong's Concordance*, s.v. Hebrew 3068 *Yhvh*, http://biblesuite.com /hebrew/3068.htm.

19. *Strong's Concordance*, s.v. Hebrew 5828 *ezer*, http://biblesuite.com /hebrew/5828.htm.

20. *Strong's Concordance*, s.v. Hebrew 5048 *neged*, http://biblesuite.com /hebrew/5048.htm.

21. Charles Templeton, *Farewell to God* (Toronto: McClelland and Stewart, 1996), http://books.google.com/books?id=NvTR05fodqYC &printsec=frontcover&dq=farewell+to+god&hl=en&sa=X&ei=Xtd6U brxAsaKrAGgroHgBg&ved=0CDIQ6AEwAA.

22. Eleanor Roosevelt, as quoted in *Reader's Digest*, September 1940, 37:84.

Chapter 3

1. Allan R. Gold, "Garbage Collectors Threaten a Strike in New York," *The New York Times*, November 28, 1990, http://www.nytimes .com/1990/11/28/nyregion/garbage-collectors-threaten-a-strike-in-

new-york.html; and Sewell Chan, "Manhattan: Garbage Strike Ends," *The New York Times*, August 06, 2006, http://www.nytimes.com /2006/08/03/nyregion/03mbrfs-001.html.

Chapter 4

1. The Pew Forum on Religion and Public Life, *US Religious Landscape Survey*, "The Stronger Sex—Spiritually Speaking," Pew Research Center, February 26, 2009, http://www.pewforum.org/The-Stronger-Sex----Spiritually-Speaking.aspx.
2. *Strong's Concordance*, s.v. Greek 3056 *logos*, http://biblesuite.com /greek/3056.htm.
3. *Strong's Concordance*, s.v. Greek 4487 *rhema,* http://biblesuite.com /greek/4487.htm.
4. Author unknown, though often attributed to Dr. Seuss. For more information, see William H. Shepherd, *Without a Net: Preaching in the Paperless Pulpit* (Lima, OH: CSS Publishing, 2004), 164–165.

Chapter 5

1. Darrel Bock, *Baker Exegetical Commentary on the New Testament* (Grand Rapids, MI: Baker Academic, 1994), 607-608.

Chapter 6

1. William Law, *The Works of the Reverend William Law* (London: J. Richardson, 1762), 74.

Chapter 7

1. *Strong's Concordance*, s.v. Hebrew 1136 *chesed*, http://biblesuite.com /hebrew/1136.htm.
2. Aline Reynolds, "One Survivor from 9/11 Returns Home, for Good," *Downtown Express,* December 29, 2010, http://www.downtownexpress .com/de_401/onesurvivor.html; and Associated Press, "9/11 'Survivor Tree' Blossoms at Start of Spring," NBC New York, March 20, 2012, http://www.nbcnewyork.com/news/local/911-Survivor-Tree-World-Trade-Center-Pear-Tree-Ground-Zero-Blossoms-Spring-143548806 .html.

Chapter 8

1. *Strong's Concordance*, s.v. Greek 5299 *hypopiazo*, http://biblesuite.com /greek/5299.htm.

Chapter 9

1. Corrie ten Boom, John Sherrill and Elizabeth Sherrill, *The Hiding Place* (Peabody, MA: Hendrickson, 1971), 240.
2. Michael Zigarelli, "Distracted from God: A Five-Year Worldwide Study," in *Christianity 9 to 5*, http://www.epiphanyresources.com/9to5/articles/distractedfromgod.htm.
3. Charles R. Swindoll, as quoted on GoodReads, http://www.goodreads.com/author/quotes/5139.Charles_R_Swindoll.

Chapter 11

1. *Strong's Concordance*, s.v. Greek 1577 *ecclesia*, http://biblesuite.com/greek/1577.htm.
2. See Genesis 23:9–10, 17–18; Joshua 20:4; Judges 9:35; and Deuteronomy 21:19; 25:7.
3. *Strong's Concordance*, s.v. Greek 444 *anthropos*, http://biblesuite.com/greek/444.htm.

Chapter 12

1. Jennifer Rosenberg, "Rosa Parks Refuses to Give Up Her Bus Seat," accessed April 25, 2013, http://history1900s.about.com/od/1950s/qt/RosaParks.htm; Facing History and Ourselves, "A Pivotal Moment in the Civil Rights Movement: The Murder of Emmett Till," http://www.facinghistory.org/resources/units/pivotal-moment-civil-rights-movemet; Christopher Klein, "10 Things You May Not Know About Rosa Parks," History.com, February 4, 2013, http://www.history.com/news/10-things-you-may-not-know-about-rosa-parks; and "The Montgomery Bus Boycott: December 5, 1955–December 26, 1956," accessed April 30, 2013, http://webcache.googleusercontent.com/search?q=cache:UIdWWXUT3boJ:www3.pittsfield.net/groups/parkerchandler/wiki/welcome/attachments/135be/Bus%2520Boycott%2520Begins.docx+rosa+parks+row+eleven&cd=1&hl=en&ct=clnk&gl=us&client=safari.